Coming Forth As Gold
TRUSTING GOD
THROUGH THE PROCESS
TO RECEIVE WHAT HE PROMISED

CHARLENE GARDNER

iUniverse LLC
Bloomington

"COMING FORTH AS GOLD" TRUSTING GOD THROUGH THE PROCESS TO RECEIVE WHAT HE PROMISED

iUniverse books may be ordered through booksellers or by contacting:

iUniverse
1663 Liberty Drive
Bloomington, IN 47403
www.iuniverse.com
1-800-Authors (1-800-288-4677)

ISBN: 978-1-4917-2241-1 (sc)
ISBN: 978-1-4917-2242-8 (e)

Printed in the United States of America.

iUniverse rev. date: 3/10/2014

Contents

Preface

Life is filled with many intricate details of suffering and joy. We don't always understand the "why" that accompanies our trouble. We carry through life "season tickets" and we all with set expectations stand in visible and invisible lines waiting for the next carousel of events to unfold. The writing on the tickets is always there, but many times the smaller print on them conveys messages that we just weren't prepared to see. Nevertheless, one thing is for sure, God has a strategy of purpose in our pain. God by His manifold grace can recycle our appalling situations into treasures of wisdom for us and others. God's intentions for our lives stretch with love beyond the skies to bring us to an open field of hope. The Scripture declares, "And we know that all things work together for good to them that love God, to them who are the called according to his purpose" (Romans 8:28).

One day while thinking over my life and trying to make some sense out what I was presently facing, I sat on the bed and said, "Lord, why do I have to go through so much?" (Sound familiar?). No answer came right away as I wondered in complete silence, and continued in my daily activities. At the closing of the day I bowed down to thank the Lord and went to bed. While in a deep sleep, I had a dream and I believe that it was connected to the question that I had asked Him earlier in the day. The dream—with its interpretation is what I would like to share with you.

As you read this book, I pray the Holy Spirit would inspire you to persevere in this race as a "good soldier of Jesus Christ." I hope that your heart will be enlightened as fresh perspectives are imparted into your spirit. No, this book doesn't have all the answers. It's not an easy manual of take three steps and your out. Rather, it is a message designed to speak from heart to heart and to encourage the believer in their Christian walk concerning endurance, experience, and enrichment. I have learned out of my own brokenness that there is healing in the revealing of God's truth.

Beloved, know that God has everything under His care. The Kingdom is in control! We serve the God who has our best interest at heart. As we go through the storm, we continue to learn by faith to embrace His powerful peace even when there is seems to be no explanation. Then when the storm has subsided, radiant joy and the beauty of the Lord will rest upon you. So if we don't faint before the finish we shall, "Come Forth As Gold"!

Dedication

This book is dedicated in loving memory to my precious mother Gladys Marie Martin (now deceased). I will always cherish my thoughts of her who consistently prayed and cared for her children. Her beauty and grace shall never be forgotten. Her spiritual legacy lives on in all her children. One of her favorite songs that we enjoyed hearing her sing was, *"Just a Little More Faith and Grace, That's all I Need."*

PART ONE

The Dream Story Told

CHAPTER ONE

Invitation to the Plant

But He knows the way that I take; When he has tested me, I shall come forth as gold.
Job 23:10 (NKJ)

One tranquil morning I, May Crossover (my name) was sitting in my living room looking out the window at the graceful mountains of Colorado, contemplating the day ahead. As I sat, the golden sun, beaming through my windows warmed me while I collected my thoughts. Then I heard a telephone ring in the distance; I answered, and to my delight it was Boss, my dear friend with whom I often had fellowship with. Boss was the proprietor CEO of a refinery called, "Golden Hearts INC". Boss had called to invite me to tour his plant and witness his handiwork. I respectfully admired and appreciated him because he was so full of wisdom and sound judgment. I looked expectantly to him; and not merely because of his great wealth, but for who he was.

The place where Boss managed was a unique, state-of-the-ark operational structure that involved the transformation of a trained people who were called to a mission that would effect their generation. These peculiar people whom Boss selected came from all walks of life and varied in race, gender and age. They were confined into a holding area while waiting to be made into gold. The people waited anxiously for Boss to call them out one by one to go through the tedious but rewarding process.

When I arrived, and walked into his warehouse, the first thing that I encountered was an intense heat that masked my being and sapped my strength. The dichotomy of this place rendered itself dreadful and yet somehow intriguing. I understood that the heat factor was central to the conditioning of the vessels, which were being molded in preparation for the coming phases that they would endure.

Boss beckoned me to the side and said, "Today, you will witness one of my subjects, Mr. Will B. Dunn, transform into fine gold. This is what I desire for him for my noble purpose." "Mr. Dunn!" Boss thundered, "Take off your clothes and gird up your mind. Your time is at hand. Only, be thou strong." Then he turned aside to look me square in my eyes and ordered, "May, my special friend, there is to be no interference at anytime during the course of events. Is that understood?" I submitted, "Yes, Sir."

At this point, we (others were on the tour as well) looked to see who Mr. Will B. Dunn was? Then, timorously ambling through the crowd was a short, bald man with fair skin and a medium build. He looked up at Boss. Not a word was spoken between them, only a nod of the head and a gentle smile. One could discern that the man was willing but uncertain of how all this would take place. Nevertheless, his entire life was now in the capable hands of Boss.

I noticed that at the same time Mr. Dunn was stepping forward, there was also a human-like male robot, designed by Boss coming across the room to pick him up. Boss called him, Helper. Helper's artistic and qualitative look was of solid, purified silver and gold. He was strong and comforting–capable and sensitive. He did not speak of himself, nor did he speak a word to Mr. Dunn for the time being. His only commission was to gladly obey Boss with fidelity, as well as to assist those who had been pre-selected for the process.

Helper had a built-in timing-mechanism for each individual within the plant. It was precise and well synchronized according to Boss's time. A certain amount of time was allotted for every level of the process, the length of time varying for each person. No one would stay for too long or too short.

Helper came and lifted Mr. Dunn. Although he was somewhat frantic, he wouldn't fight the Helper who carried him to an area where there were enormous industrious kettles. With great care, he slowly submerged Mr. Dunn in the first kettle, a cistern of nothing but pure boiling Olive Oil.

I shivered as I watched him endure the pain and the heat of the oil. Mr. Dunn screamed at the top of his voice, but there was nothing anyone could do. In my heart I wanted to rescue him and say to Boss, "Enough is enough! You have already taken this too far and you claim this is only the beginning! How can anyone be put through this sheer terror? What is wrong with you Boss?"

Boss looked at me as though he was reading my every thought, then replied, "I'm in control! Don't allow yourself to think unjustly of me. They all must go the way appointed for them. I hold their best interest in my integrity, and as agonizing as this may be, the results will be phenomenal. I will not forsake them." Boss, with words few – ever so gracious, had a way of settling my spirit and the atmosphere. Even though I had some misguided suspicious of him, somehow in my heart I still respected his authority – being helplessly attracted to him I trusted his decision, and I believed his heart was blameless.

Finally, the timer went off within Helper, making a loud beeping sound. I could imagine that to Mr. Will B. Dunn, it seemed like an eternity. Helper pulled him out of the kettle and rushed him to another section where workers in the plant assisted. The workers in this section were called the "Shearers".

The "Shearers" were an anonymous group of people whose job was to stand by quietly and await the people coming from the oil, with sharp knives to peel off their flesh. The oil from the previous process saturates the skin through and through, thereby making it soft and pliable. The "Shearers" stripped off Mr. Dunn's flesh, only leaving a thin layer of skin on so that everything inside would remain sealed. Only the inner man was now available for the duration of the process. Mr. Dunn sat still and allowed them to complete the work at hand. He did not scream this time or move as the tears trickled down what was left of his sad face. He never said a mumbling word.

When the shearing was finished, Helper came to pick him up and carry him to the second kettle. It was similar to the first in size, but its contents consisted of boiling, liquefied gold, glistening and beautiful. The same process was repeated. Helper puts him in slowly. The timer is set, and the gold saturated his entire being. After a while, the timer went off and Helper withdrew his gold drenched-body from the kettle.

Strait way, Helper took Mr. Dunn to a large waiting room with wax paper covering the floor and gently laid him down in a corner. At this time, he found himself suddenly and utterly alone. The sound proof waiting room was void of all activity. Boss came into the calm atmosphere of the room, but only for a few minutes, standing looking at Mr. Will B. Dunn with compassion in his eyes. He spoke softly, "Wait on me and your heart shall be strengthened. (Psalm 27:14) I know that I have hidden you in obscurity presently, but know, my son, that I am with you. In quietness and in confidence shall be your strength. (Isaiah 30:15b). The gold is not only on you but is working in you, producing a royal heart and righteous character." After he spoke those words, he quietly closed the door behind him.

It seemed as though Mr. Dunn was totally isolated, lying there, feeling like a dead man forgotten and out of mind. I pensively said to myself, "These peculiar people really want to be used in a special way." Boss told them, "Whosoever is willing let him come." I'm sure some came with a glad heart without considering the high and virtuous standard that would be required of them. Because the process is costly, others probably heard and turned back–letting the "price tag" change their minds. However, the blessed exchange, of giving up the lesser for the greater has an "eternal weight of glory", and deep down in my heart I believed it was worth it!"

Several hours had passed by before Helper made his way back to the waiting room. He picked up Mr. Dunn very carefully, and off they went. After they left, a janitor came by to take the portion of wax paper that Mr. Dunn was on and placed the excess gold which dripped from him back into the tank of gold for the next person. Their next stop as I followed close behind, was the "Refiner's Fire."

This particular area, being the most heated of all throughout the plant, was also the most mystical and apprehensive place. I say mystical, because of the heat's ability to purify, enlighten, and transform; apprehensive because of the unpleasantness of test and affliction.

When we entered this room, there sat in the middle of the floor an old fashioned, black iron furnace, tall with a wide and deep base. I noticed that the inferno had already been ignited. The flames were kindling high, the sound was like small crackling fireworks, and the radiant colors were a combination of orange, red, and yellow. Yet in all of this, I observed that flames were not out of control but rather tempered with vigorous consistency.

Poor Mr. Dunn, exasperated, looking in the face of Helper dramatically expressed as they got closer to the fire: "Don't even think about trying to put me in there! Boss wouldn't allow any more on me than I could bear, or would he? Doesn't he care? What's the purpose of all this "stretching" my soul? Couldn't we just evade this part and move on?" Helper, still holding him in his arms said nothing, He only looked intently in Mr. Dunn's eyes with love and comfort.

Mr. Dunn knew in his heart that this phase was a vital part of his transformation. So he dropped his head, and gave up the struggle as a sign of inward submission and in a weak tone he uttered, "For I know that my redeemer lives, and He shall stand at last upon the earth." (Job 19:25). As Helper began walking toward the furnace, Mr. Dunn shrunk back with craven fear, for it suddenly dawned on him that in every facet of the process, there involves a higher degree of heat, and this it appeared to be the ultimate. He took a deep breath, closed his eyes and faintly continued saying, "Though he slay me, yet will I trust Him." (Job 13:15). He went into the fire and the door was shut!

I grieved for him, seeing that he had already endured so much. My own reasoning warred within me, suggesting to me that just maybe Mr. Dunn is finished. Still, in my heart there was hope. Hope that he would come out of this as Boss promised. Hope! It is a word that our ears love to hear and our eyes love to see manifested. What does it mean to me? It means: H-Healing O-Opportunity P-Provision E-Expectation, it's a proclaiming hope that at the latter end he would rise above all that he had suffered and be greatly increased. We waited patiently and that hope was quickened in us when we heard the beeper going off again for the last time.

When Helper opened the furnace door, the heat overwhelmed us, and we began gasping for fresh air and water. Our eyes strained as we gazed through the smoke, beholding Mr. Dunn walking out of the fire. His body was solid like an outer armor and it sparkled like a diamond in the twilight. His determined face was set like a flint no longer looking distressed. Now, instead of exhibiting cowardice, he only exuded confidence. His continence was beautifully filled with light, it was captivating to look at him and interestingly there was no smell of smoke upon him. He glanced at us with a glimmer in his eyes and a liberating smile that indicated to us that he was alright.

I thought the process was concluded, but there was one more stop before being presented to Boss. This intriguing stop was on a completely different side of the plant described as the "Pool of Refreshing". The closer I got to the pool, the more I sensed something new and festive about to take place. I shook off the heaviness that weighed me down like an eagle plucking off his soiled feathers, waiting for new ones to grow. With my strength renewed, I opened the butterfly glass stained double doors and sunlight shined forth through the bay windows. I felt a fresh breeze caress my face. The aroma of this place was like sweet perfume and surrounding the pool was a host of lovely plants and blooming flowers. The contour of blue water was still and peaceful as if it were awaiting someone to occupy the waters.

Helper assisted Mr. Dunn easily into the pool, and as he went down, steam began to arise from the water on contact with his body. The steam filled the room quickly, like a pleasant mist coming from an ocean. While watching Mr. Dunn's face, one could see a release of tension being relieved from him as he sat there relaxing in the cool water.

I heard him humbly whisper, "All the days of my appointed time will I wait till my change comes." (Job 14:14) "Praise to my Redeemer, my change has finally come. I can see the breaking of day. I see now that this was needful for me. I was so undone, depending on my own strength to produce something of worth. It was working for my good, even though there were times when I felt like giving up. Boss's ways and intentions were mightier than my own. I could see the progress that was made, even in the midst of so much pressure."

Helper came around with an expression of joy on his face and a towel in his hand as he took Mr. Dunn out of the water and dried him. Glistening in the sunlight, he was pure, firm, and made whole from the inside out. Helper led him to a mirror to see himself and while he stood there in awe, examining his new man, tears filled his eyes.

Helper inquired of him, "Are you ready?" Mr. Will B. Dunn replied, "Yes, I'm ready." This time Helper did not carry him, they walked side-by-side down a long hall briefly conversing about the things that took place. I heard Helper ask Mr. Dunn to wait in the hall. He walked ahead of him into the entrance of Boss's chambers. He announced, "The process of substance is completed as you have desired Sir, and your chosen vessel is prepared for your service." Boss answered, "Well of course! Send him in at once!" Helper beckoned Mr. Dunn to come in. He walked in and stood looking at Boss with his eyebrows raised high because for the first time, he was seeing Boss differently.

As Mr. Dunn came closer, he rejoiced with great alacrity in Boss's presence, both humbled and honored. Mr. Dunn said, "Here am I." Boss looked at him with a gorgeous smile then with assurance stated, "I'm pleased. I can see my reflection just as I am, in you." You see, during the process, Boss was fully dressed and we couldn't behold his golden glory. But afterward, sitting in his chamber, transfiguration occurred and we saw his splendid riches of glory. Later, I found out that Boss went through a more agonizing process than anyone could ever go through, which explains why Mr. Dunn saw him so differently. Boss further proclaimed, "And they shall be mine says the Lord of hosts, in that day when I make up my jewels; and will spare them, as a man spares his own son that serves him." (Malachi 3:17).

"My eyes were upon you the whole time, and I know you didn't fully understand the meaning, but now you will. I know that you were perplexed, but I never left you in despair. Don't ever doubt my love for you. It is an everlasting love. And by the way, you did have a constant companion, Helper, who was assigned to lead, hold, and help you every step of the way. At each stage where you surrendered to my agenda, the oil increased upon you making it your reality more possible for the work you must now do. Now my son, unite with me and let us build together the furtherance of my plan in the earth. Let us also help others to come through the "Refiner's Fire" as gold. Enter into my joy!"

PART TWO

The Dream Story Unfolds

CHAPTER TWO
Selected and Tailored Made

"Of His own will He brought us forth by the word of truth, that
we might be a kind of firstfruits of His creatures."
James 1:18

Let us now transition from the allegory to the relative. In the beginning of the story we find a people who have been chosen for a purpose. When we think of someone or something being selected for a special reason, there is a sense of honor and dignity associated to the nominee. Now concerning the selection of God, we must understand that He has hand picked us out before the foundation of the world. The selection indicates that careful and skillful consideration has been appropriated to the person or elements involved. He has bought us with His precious blood therefore, we are not our own, we belong to Him (I Corinthians 6:19-20). We have been selected to serve someone, to be somebody, and to go somewhere according to the blue print of God. In His infinite wisdom He has prepared a people of every kindred, tongue, and nation that will know Him.

"Ye have not chosen me, but I have chosen you, and ordained you, that ye should go
and bring forth fruit, and that your fruit should remain: that whatsoever ye shall ask of
the Father in my name, he may give you" (John 15:16). KJV

It's encouraging to know that the Scripture declares, "Of His own will He brought us forth by the word of truth." (James 1:18) In other words, He desired us out of His own volition and generous love to be reconciled unto Himself through His son Jesus Christ. It was not by force or done begrudgingly, it was not by a lie forged from Satan or the world's estimation of you and I, but by the **truth**. God's truth is uncontaminated.

It affords us the grace to be real and live in reality. The truth makes us free, changes our lives, and is eternal. Jesus said, *"I am the way, the truth, and the life. No one comes to the Father except through Me"* (John 14:6).

"For ye have not received the spirit of bondage again to fear; but ye have received the Spirit of adoption, whereby we cry, Abba, Father" (Romans 8:15).

Adoption is wonderful because it is by choice that one is legally taken into a family. Total acceptance is a prerequisite for adoption, therefore, rejection should have no residence in a family that is adopting. Now that doesn't mean that the person adopted will not encounter rejection during their life span, but the root of it doesn't have to remain because acceptance has canceled it out.

Rejection Doesn't Live Here Anymore

Many people including Christians have been tormented and haunted by rejection. Rejection is like poisonous arrows shot in your heart and mind to disparage you and assassin your self-esteem, which will result in isolation and suspicions.

Growing up in my early teens even into some of my adult age, I tolerated the root of rejection in my life. I was raised in a Christian home with a godly mother, who taught us biblical principals to stand upon. But the enemy sought to elude my mind from even the concept of acceptance. He wielded his attacks through various circumstances and through loneliness which opened the door to this rejection. When we don't know who we are and Whom we belong to, the stranger's voice comes in and suggests seducing lies of what he wants us to be. **Warning: Keep Away From the Stranger!**

Rejection caused me to beat myself down and projected an illegal permission for others to do the same. I was trapped by fear and false reasoning that kept me from loving others and myself. It ruled my life and prohibited me from looking through the eyes of love and faith. Because the root of rejection was at work in my life, even when people did like and accept me, I would look at them with suspicion and expect them to reject me sooner or later. The spirit of rejection caused me to have a poor reflection of myself which lead to poor perception. I would tell myself: "If only I were interesting enough to be invited, pretty enough to be picked, diverse enough to be desired, good enough to be wanted, and anointed enough to be allowed, everything would be all right". Have you ever felt that way or even worse—believed that way?

This relentless cycle went on until I got severely tired. I cried out unto my God for complete deliverance from the root of rejection. I began to wash myself with the power of His Word and started believing in His unfailing, unconditional, and unlimited love for me. The songwriter wrote, "When nothing else could help, love lifted me." Christ ministered to me the healing balm of His acceptance and love. Through the process of time along with meditation on the Word, I overcame the root of rejection and its negative affect on my life.

If this stronghold binds you, you too can be set free today. It makes no difference what adversities you have faced or how many people have dropped out of your life. When people drop out, the promises of God yet remain. Personally, I would like to say: "I'm sorry that you encountered some rejection on today. It came to intimidate you; it came to back you into a corner. However, the beauty of your spirit stood tall against it. Beloved, I know that there are times when you didn't feel like grappling with the waves of challenge or walking on the gravel of difficulty. Yet your determination was set like ivory to defend you. Having peace with God and yourself made it possible. The essence of who you are sings the sweet melody of honor and value. Take courage from this day forward and know that you are amazingly significant!" Paul reveals some liberating news to us in the book of Ephesians 1:5-6.

> *"Having predestined us to adoption as sons by Jesus Christ to Himself, according to the good pleasure of His will, to the praise of the glory of His grace, by which He has made us accepted in the Beloved."*

Rest and partake of this Word, knowing that in advance this was decreed through the mouth and the work of God. You and I have already been fit or "tailored- made" into His body; the measurements of grace and faith have been taken for you. He knows the boundaries of how far you can go, how high you can reach, and how much you can stretch. Your depth in Him has already been predetermined; marvelous are His thoughts towards us!

Truth to Consider

God has made us in His image. One by one we are uniquely hand crafted by design. When we accepted Christ He set us free to accept others and love them. People don't have to conform to our way of thinking or our way of doing things. Everyone is different, and they have been called to conform to the image of Christ. Be what God intended you to be and He will perfect that which concerns you. (See Psalm 138:8). He knows our ending as well as our beginning.

What about the past, some might ask? Simply put, in His mercy He covered it in the blood. Determine in your mind to refuse being driven by guilt to make up for past mistakes. Let people know that you don't have a ticket for the "guilt trip", the flight is fully booked and there is no room for you. Don't look behind you but ahead, because the past cannot be trusted. It can be likened unto medicine that has been expired. If you take it in disregard to the expiration date for pain, its potency might be dissipated and will not work. You are now taking something at your own risk, which may create another unexpected ailment. How many today are living in the now but are still taking pills of the past for their pain, only creating other problems? Stop telling yourself, "I just cannot get over this." "Do you hear the words that are coming out of your mouth?" With the help of Christ you can get over whatever your "this" may be. For this to shall pass.

Most of the time we have to cough the past up as an experience and walk on to new heights in God. I know that there are people who will <u>try</u> to keep you attached to your past by reminding you of it. Why? Could it be because of their unbelief to the power of Christ's ability to change you? Christ forgave you when you repented and He also gave you the strength to forgive yourself. Now I implore you to stay free and stand firm on this Word, *"Therefore if any man be in Christ, he is a new creature; old things are past away; behold, all things are become new"* (II Corinthians 5:17).

Each day that we wake up in the morning we should thank God for Who He is and celebrate who we are in Him. Know that we are greatly loved, "Selected, and Tailored-made" for such a time as this.

CHAPTER THREE

The Boiling Oil

"But my horn You have exalted like a wild ox; I have been anointed with fresh oil".
Psalm *92:10*

The anointing is a special operative power placed in and upon a person by the Holy Spirit to fulfill a specific task or mission. I have heard the statement: "The anointing makes it easy"; and it most certainly does. But not only that, it demonstrates the power of God to bring life and healing. The anointing initiates true change in a believer's life and dynamically influences them to good works. It is more than just a good feeling, more than a quick wave of the Spirit, but the anointing of God comes to empower us for Kingdom business in everyday living.

Anointing oil is made mostly from olives that have been beaten and crushed with a stone grinder. In Old Testament times, it was deemed as being purely consecrated for the holy things of God. It was so precious that it had to be respected and protected by whom it had been placed upon.

"Then the Lord spoke to Moses, saying: Command the children of Israel that they bring to you pure oil of pressed olives for the light, to make the lamps burn continually."
(Leviticus 24:1–2)

Note that this pure oil was "pressed" or in the KJV "beaten". Christ the Anointed One, was pressed in the Garden of Gethsemane (see Luke 22:39–42), and was beaten before He was crucified on the cross (see Matthew 27:26). We are compelled to follow in His steps, though we are pressed on every side and have encountered some beatings of our own. Nevertheless, it is crucial that we conserve fresh oil in our vessel through the gift of the Holy Spirit; as a matter of fact, the more we are pressed for Christ's sake, more oil is generated. It is the Holy Spirit that keeps our heart ablaze even when we run into the cold places of life. As we continue to dwell in the Anointed One, He will anoint our heads with oil and the oil will run down to destroy the yoke and relieve the anxious mind.

The purpose for the oil in the previous verse was for light in order for the lamps to burn continually. The word burn here, doesn't connote being consumed or to undergo combustion. However, in the Hebrew the word is *alah* that means "to go up, ascend, or offer up." The Lord wanted the light in the lamps to go up continually. Not flickering, not going out and coming back in but to abide.

Jesus, being the perpetual Light of the world calls us the light of the world, "a city that is set on a hill cannot be hidden" (Matthew 5:14). We need light to see clearly that our steps may be guided. We need light to shine forth in the dark places of men's hearts. The light must ascend in the home, on the job, even in the church. We can abide in the light by: Not being weary of the Lords of correction; Walking in the light that has been sown; Waiting on the Lord for His wisdom and council; and by Warring effectively in the Spirit by the Word.

Appreciate the Anointing

True repentance from the heart helps us to walk softly before the Lord. It also enhances our ability to be sensitive and pliable in the hands of God. This in turn helps us to accept the responsibility that comes with a special anointing. If we intend to have the anointing rest on our lives one of the requirements is that we must have a teachable spirit. The revelation of Jesus Christ being received and applied to our lives results in fresh oil being released to us. We are to learn how to flow within the dynamics of the anointing, because it is such a liberating substance.

Did you know that the anointing has an appetite? We are encouraged to feed and not deprive it. We feed it by spending adequate time in the presence of the Lord. Its not about religion but an intimate relationship with the Father compelling us to have a separated life unto God in holiness, obedience to the Word, and worship to the living God. Its appetite calls for the spirit of humility, which stimulates us to **value** the anointing of God. In the allegory, it took humility for Mr. Dunn to be dipped into the "boiling oil". Humility is the repeated step that takes us higher and higher because it broadens us to be more resourceful. Humility aids to protect your internal values. Proverbs 22:4 declares: *"By humility and the fear of the Lord are riches and honor and life."* Keep in mind that humility is a tremendous asset in the sight of the Lord.

The anointing does not rest on the proud who think they can do anything, or live any kind of way. King Saul is a prime example of living in a presumptuous state, taking the commands of the Lord for granted and disobeying them. I love Saul's beginning, but his ending is sorrowfully tragic.

> *"So Samuel said, "When you were little in your own eyes, were you not head of the tribes of Israel? And did not the Lord anoint you king over Israel? Now the Lord sent you on a mission, and said, "Go and utterly destroy the sinners, the Amalekites, and fight against them until they are consumed." Why then did you not obey the voice of the Lord? Why did you swoop down on the spoil, and do evil in the sight of the Lord?"*
> (I Samuel 15:17-19).

For every level of the anointing, there are commands that must be followed, and when they are, we will remain in a prepared place for God to use us. When King David had committed adultery with Bath-Sheba and murdered her husband Uriah the Hittite with the sword, the Lord sent Nathan to tell him a story that represented David's own actions.

> *"And Nathan said to David, Thou art the man. Thus saith the Lord God of Israel, I anointed thee to be king over Israel, and I delivered thee out of the hand of Saul;"* (II Samuel 12:7).

When Saul and David had fallen prey by compromising their stand with the Lord, what is the first thing that the Lord brings back to their memory? He reminded them of the **anointing that He put upon their life.** To the Lord this was no light thing, because He had chosen them to be carriers of His operative deliverance for the people. The Spirit of the Lord departed from Saul, but restoration was granted to David through true repentance. A gift may pacify an offense, but repentance will produce an acceptable offering.

King Saul not only sowed a dishonorable exchange for his soul; he also caused an abrupt dismissal of the precious anointing. Contamination will always hinder the flow of the anointing. Why are so many forfeiting the yoke destroying power of God by pride and foolishness? Could it be that they're operating in a residue of their past fellowship with God and overriding the fact that repentance is the way back to the true power Source. I have seen great men and women fall due to this very thing, they are the 21st Century Saul's of our day. Instead of repenting and getting healed, they kept running and tripped headlong over their unresolved issues.

It is even sad to say that some will even try to imitate what God has given to another person. They want what they see in operation, but fail to allow God to prove their character (we will discuss more about character in Chapter Seven). They will treasure an aggrandizing reputation without giving thought of taking up their cross. Soon they realize that the oil of God is found resting on lives that have a valid relationship with the Lord. Only when we turn our hearts back to God with a broken and contrite spirit, will the power surge of the Spirit be poured out upon us..

Today we have prestigious buildings, melodious choirs, exciting praise teams, and radical preaching; however, if the anointing of the Spirit is not present, what will it really accomplish? It's the anointing of Christ that makes an effective difference in our lives.

What the church and people outside the church need now is not another hero but anointed vessels. We need vessels who are willing to pay a price for God to use them; broken vessels who will allow the holy oil to flow freely from their hearts. Make no mistake about it beloved, we will walk the cost out for the anointing in dedication, suffering, obedience, and consecration. This is what it will take to increase and keep it.

My Cup Runs Over

The anointing is a teacher. It teaches us all things and it is true and not a lie. It teaches us to abide in Him, walking worthy and having fruitful lives. (See 1John 2:27). I firmly believe that it's the Word and the anointing together that are going to usher us into the next realm of His glory. If we continue to believe on Him as the Scriptures has said, "then out of your belly shall flow rivers of living waters" (John 7:38b).

Yes, we need the anointing and beside it we need the rivers flowing. This flow comes from believing and acting upon the implanted Word, which ripples in our hearts by the Holy Spirit. We need not to dry out and fold up because the Living Water, Who is Jesus, will quench our thirsty souls. Even when we come across parched places in our lives, just call on His name, believe the Scriptures and get ready to be inundated with the rivers of life.

Everywhere Jesus went He was prepared to release the power of God and we are commissioned to do the same. I know that there are times in our human frailty when we don't "feel" like serving or pressing our way to help someone else in need. However, when I consider the life of Christ, I'm quickly reminded of what He said in Luke chapter 4 verses 18-19: *"The Spirit of the Lord is upon me, because he has anointed me to preach the gospel to the poor; he has sent me to heal the broken hearted, to preach deliverance to the captives, and recovering sight to the blind, to set at liberty them that are bruised, to preach the acceptable year of the Lord."* Wow! Talk about a loving and unceasing "to do list" our Lord's work tops them all. And if that isn't enough, look in Acts chapter 10 verse 38, *"How God anointed Jesus of Nazareth with the Holy Spirit and with power, who went about doing good and healing all who were oppressed by the devil, for God was with Him."* He keeps on giving until the very end. He enables us by His grace and strength to keep giving through Him. It's quite evident that the anointing is very active and used to benefit others.

Just when I thought I was out of oil to give, another supply would profuse out and satisfy the needy soul. So anyone, who is reading this chapter and have considered throwing in the towel because the load is a little too heavy, and weariness has become your bosom buddy, may I gently advise you to come unto Him; for He will give you rest for your soul. Bear in mind that every time you pour out, go back to the Source and allow Him to refresh you again. The Anointed One will lubricate every part of your being and your cup will run over to the next person who needs a touch of fresh oil from on high.

CHAPTER FOUR

The Place of the Shearers

"Therefore we also, since we are surrounded by so great a cloud of witnesses,
let us lay aside every weight, and the sin which so easily ensnares us,
and let us run with endurance the race that is set before us".
Hebrews 12:1

The precious oil of the anointing thoroughly working in us, will also condition us to shed off weights and sin that impedes our walk with the Lord. That's why the Good Shepherd, in His infinite wisdom, leads us into stages of spiritual shedding in order for His children to advance into Christlikeness.

Jesus said, *"It is the Spirit that quickeneth; the flesh profiteth nothing. The word that I speak unto you, they are spirit, and they are life" (John 6:63)* KJV. God's Word is a cleansing agent that must be implemented in our lives to wash us from all "filthiness of the flesh and spirit". The Word makes acute incisions into the heart and mind, freeing us from wrong attitudes, secret agendas, impure thoughts, and wrong motives just to name a few.

Once or twice a year, sheep must be sheared from their thick, heavy wool. The shearing prevents parasites from lodging in their wool and causes them to be less susceptible to disease. They are light and free to play because the heaviness has been lifted off of them. It is the same way with us, the sheep of His pasture. If there is no shearing, the entanglements of this life with its heavy pressures will pine away at our spiritual lives, this making us susceptible to the disease of sin.

"For the word of God is quick, and powerful, sharper than any two-edged sword, piercing
even to the dividing asunder of soul and spirit, and of the joints and the morrow, and is
a discerner of the thoughts and intents of the heart" (Hebrews 4:12). KJV

The Divine Physician has made all things ready. Will we trust Him and go under the knife? He is greatly skilled. His credibility as Chief Surgeon is immaculately irrefutable. He cuts out and transplants in – He has torn, but He will bind us with healing sutures. As we are being molded on the operating table, we will put on and put off, always making room for new things.

A child will want to hold on to a hundred old toys, and as a result, his toy chest cannot contain any new toys because there is no room. God is doing a new thing throughout the earth and He wants His children to be very much apart of the plan, but the problem is some of the old patterns, "our way of doings things" is still hanging around. Let us consent today for Him to take away the unprofitable things that we are clutching on to. He desires an enlarged-hearted people who are willing to make room for the new at His command; for the enriched season of blessings along with signs and wonders are upon us now.

Breaking Up the Hard Ground

As a child growing up, I watched my mother plant a variety of vegetables in our backyard garden in the summer time. Periodically, she would go out back and see some weeds growing next to the flourishing green plants. I observed that she would not pull up the weeds right away because she wanted to wait for a good showering of rain to fall first (during this particular summer season it rained quite often). After the rain would come, the next day, we would put on our gloves and go out to the yard to pull the weeds from the root. They were so easy to pull out due to the rain from the previous day softening the ground.

> *"My doctrine shall drop as the rain, my speech shall distill as the dew, as the small rain upon the tender herb, and as the showers upon the grass"* (Deuteronomy 32:2). KJV

When we hear the Word, it drops as the rain and breaks up the "fallow ground" of our hearts. This makes it easy for the Husbandman of our souls to pull out the poisonous weeds that will infect our harvest. Jesus revealed that, *"Every branch in Me that does not bear fruit he takes away; and every branch that bears fruit, he prunes, that it may bear more fruit"* (John 15:2).

When pruning occurs, there is a greater potential for the fruit to increase. The degree advances from–fruit, to more fruit, too much fruit. It is with much fruit that the Father is glorified. (See John 15:8). I know that a cut back doesn't feel good and to the natural eye, you appear helpless and deficient for the time being. The truth of the matter is you're on a new plain of faith. As we dare to face the dynamics of choice and hold on to God's graceful hands–the hands of Him who takes less and makes more, we will experience golden trust that leads to many possibilities. The good news is that after the pruning, new sprouts of fresh fruit will spring forth and strength will be added to you. Go ahead, take your rest in the Vine and watch the fruit come forth and flourish.

Ready–Set–Forgive!

There is another aspect of the place of the shearers that I would like to mention. It is when God, by His sovereignty, allows the indecent conduct of others to serve as a tool to wing us from the constant approval and dependency of people. He wants us to see how easily we can be moved by the subtle control people can have over us and we not know it. However, it becomes apparent when we desire to go to higher levels of awareness in Him.

The Holy Spirit has His eyes on these "touchy" areas of our lives and wants them to be buried with Christ. If we let them, these "troubling opportunities" will come to help us exercise the character of Christ in the earth. So put on you gear, inhale and exhale, lift up your hands and get ready to unite with the Lord in His exercise. See what He said in (Jeremiah 9:24 KJV)

> *"But let him that glorieth glory in this, that he understandeth and knoweth me, that I am the Lord which exercise lovingkindness, judgement, and righteousness, in the earth: for in these things I delight, saith the Lord."*

Often times we waste precious energy being **overly** concerned about what people think of us, bound by the opinions of man. The Word of Christ affirms and secures who we are and where we're going. We cannot afford to be so disarrayed at a person (s) behavior until it causes us to malfunction in the kingdom as it relates to "righteousness and peace and joy in the Holy Spirit"; not being moved by praise or persecution, favor or the faultfinding of men. (See Romans 14:17-18).

Paul, the servant of the Lord stated: *"lest Satan should take advantage of us; for we are not ignorant of his devices"* (II Corinthians 2:11). In this, I see examples in the particular lives of Paul and Jesus who had their identities rooted in the Father.

> *"On the next day much people that were come to the feast, when they heard that Jesus was coming to Jerusalem, took branches of palm, and went forth to meet him, and*

cried, Hosanna: Blessed is the King of Israel that cometh in the name of the Lord" (John 12:12-13).

"And the people stood beholding. And the rulers also with them derided him, saying, He saved others; Let him save himself, if he be Christ, the chosen of God." *"And saying, if you be the king of the Jews, save thyself"* (Luke 23:35,37). Now concerning Apostle Paul it is written: *"And when the barbarians saw the venomous beast hang on his hand, they said among themselves,* **No doubt this man is a murderer,**{emphasis added} *whom, though he hath escaped the sea, yet vengeance suffereth not to live. And he shook off the beast into the fire, and felt no harm. Howbeit they looked when he should have swollen, or fallen down dead suddenly: but after they had looked a great while, and saw no harm come to him,* **they changed their minds, and said that he was a god"** {emphasis added} (Acts 28:4-6).

People will change their mind like a pancake being turned over to the other side concerning you; but He will *"keep your mind in perfect peace when stayed on him…"* (Isaiah 26:3). This is why it is relevant for one to think soberly about himself; for one to be *"transformed by the renewing of your mind…"* (Romans 12:2). Do you look through the mirror of the Word and see yourself or do you see yourself through the expressed fickle thoughts of others?

Jesus warns his disciples by articulating: *"It is impossible but that offenses will come: but woe unto him through whom they do come!"* (Luke 17:1). The Word declares offenses will come! So prepare and *"keep yourselves in the love of God…"* (Jude 1:21). No matter how many times offense occurs, forgiveness must be the forerunner of every hurt inflicted. Peter, one of the Lord's disciples asked him, *"Lord, how often shall my brother sin against me, and I forgive him, seven times? Jesus answered him, "I say not unto you, until seven times: but seventy times seven"* (Matthew 18:21-22). It's no wonder the apostles replied back in Luke's account: "Lord, increase our faith." The command is not easy; however, it can be done through the riches of Christ's grace.

In less than four seconds I can say, "I'm going to the store." However, it may take some time for me to get there. My point is forgiveness takes time, not so much the saying of it but the process of it. How much time I believe depends on the ability to overcome, the maturity of a person, and the condition of their heart. It takes time for harassing voices to be drowned out; it takes time to stop the **rehearsal** of devastating memories, putting them to death; and it takes time for your perspective to be healed in the light of truth. Apostle Paul in his account of the stinging perils he had to undergo determinedly stated: *"Brethren, I do not count myself to have apprehended; but one thing I* *do, forgetting those things which are behind and reaching forward to those things which are ahead, I press toward the goal for the prize of the upward call of God in Christ Jesus. Therefore let us, as many as are mature have this mind; and if in anything you think otherwise, God will reveal even this to you"* (Philippians 3:13-15).

Forgiveness is advantageous even as it applies to our prayer life. I don't know about you, but I can't afford for unforgiveness to jeopardize any of my prayers. I choose to release the offender and leave them at the altar. I said to myself, "I will not let this hurt have dominion over me in Jesus name." Bitterness will try hard to raise its ugly head but I cannot allow this defilement to contaminate my spirit and make me ugly. I heard a woman say concerning her family after a hostile situation, "Forgiveness saved our lives".

"Looking diligently lest any man fail of the grace of God; lest any root of bitterness springing up trouble you, and thereby many be defiled;" (Hebrews 15:15). KJV

Forgiveness is a sacrificial gift. Often times the offender will never know how much it cost you to walk through the pain which they caused. Understand that forgiveness is not cheap, neither does it mean that you and I are weak because we forgive. Rather, it is a powerful weapon against the enemy defusing his attacks on the heart and mind. Forgiveness is a part of the ongoing growth cycle in Christ; when you stop forgiving you sabotage your growth–maturity halts. The main key in forgiveness is to continually reflect, acknowledge, and imitate the One who forgives us of our trespasses. Jesus teaches the necessity of this principle when He said: *"And whenever you stand praying, if you have anything against anyone, forgive him, that your Father in heaven may also forgive you your trespasses. But if you do not forgive, neither will your Father which is in heaven forgive your trespasses"* (Mark 11:25-26). I realized that unforgiveness is trapped pain. It will cause you to be captivated by the hurt and hold you hostage rehearsing the words and actions of people. If the pain is not released, there will be an implosion eating away like cancer in the inward parts. What must we do? Receive by faith the grace of God that has been made available unto us; for His grace will heal and enable us to let go and grow. Just as the pain was real, the healing is more real–just as the hurt was great, the healing is greater–and just as the damage was done, your healing will truly come.

We must learn how to deal with people whoever they may be, out of new mercy lest the grudges pile up. "The Lord's mercies and compassion's fail not. They are new every morning; great is His faithfulness." (See Lamentations 3:22-23). When we forgive out of His new mercy, we won't be guilty of overcharging people for their offenses. We should delight in mercy even as our heavenly Father delights in it and as we aspire to this, we will be set free to walk closer to our Lord.

Charlene Gardner

Someone Who Can Relate

It's a blessing to know that we are not alone at the place of the shearers. There is Someone Who has gone before us and has been *"…touched with the feelings of our infirmities…"* (See Hebrews 4:14). Let's take a look in the Book where Isaiah prophesied: *"He was oppressed, and he was afflicted, yet he opened not his mouth: he is brought as a lamb to the slaughter; and as a sheep before her shearers is dumb, so he opened not his mouth. Yet it pleased the Lord to bruise him; he hath put him to grief: when thou shalt make his soul an offering for sin, he shall see his seed, he shall prolong his days, and the pleasure of the Lord shall prosper in his hand. He shall see the travail of his soul, and shall be satisfied; by his knowledge shall my righteous servant justify many; for he shall bear their iniquities"* (Isaiah 53:7,10,11). KJV

It's evident in these verses that the Lord went through great agony in His suffering as His blood was poured forth for the sins of the world. And to make the sting of His assignment more complex, it "pleased the Lord to bruise Him and put Him to grief." Nothing He went through was in vain! At the end He was going to "see the travail of His soul and be satisfied". Now He's yet alive and reigns forever more to the praise of God. My gentle advice to you is, don't allow yourself to fold up and die during your time of shearing. Hold on and live to see the positive outcome of your travail, and you will be satisfied, lacking nothing.

When sheep are being sheared, there usually isn't a struggle, you may have some that try to resist at first but they eventually calm down and submit. Submission is not a blind act; it is an attitude of commitment with your eyes wide open. Submission coincides with faith, helping us to trust in the One you cannot see while actively expecting results.

Have you ever been in a situation where you wondered if the person on the "other side" was going to do right by you? As we learn from our examples, we should understand that there will be instances when someone will disregard "right" as it relates to us. But be assured that God knows how to keep the record perfectly straight. We will be comforted looking away unto Jesus and knowing that He really does identify with us at all times. Be in readiness to leave room for Him to defend us, for He will faithfully *"…maintain our right and our cause"* (Psalms 9:4).

Jesus, when before the shearers, did not open His mouth but He quietly endured the pain. Because the "Lamb was slain from the foundation of the world", He could have chose to die anytime. The chief priest, scribes, and elders always wanted to kill Him. In the garden of Gethsemane He said to them, "My soul is exceedingly sorrowful, even to death. Stay here and watch" (Mark 14:34). But He **endured** to the death of the cross and beforehand *"…committed himself to him that judgeth righteously"* (I Peter 2:23). He left His will, rights, and honor all in the hands of the Father. He was sustained by

26

knowing His Father's love for Him; knowing that He was fulfilling God's will; and He also knew who He was and where He was going (see John 13:1-3). This is what we must do, know that God loves you, know who you are, and where you are going. Endure until the end!

Well, take your rest beloved sheep in the care of the Good Shepherd, "for no man will pluck you out of His hands". Embrace courage and humbly go through your times of shearing and afterwards enter into God's sweet healing

CHAPTER FIVE

Golden Treasure

"I rejoice at Your word as one who finds great treasure."
Psalm 119:162

Coming up as a child the Easter Holiday was very special to me. I relished this occasion for two reasons: first, because of what my mother inculcated to me through the Scriptures about the resurrection of Jesus Christ. She wanted me to know that the God we serve is not dead, but yet alive–He is alive in power, majesty, dominion, and glory. Mother told me that if we would welcome Him in our hearts with gladness, He would live there by faith. When speaking about her Lord, mother spoke with so much passion and authority, for she loved Him with all her heart. When she spoke of these things, it made me feel warm inside, and I liked the idea of Someone with power and love living inside my heart.

Secondly, my mother made every effort to prepare and elate my heart for the joyous day set before us. Mother would pick out lovely apparel for my siblings and me to wear on Easter Sunday morning. I would have a "Shirley Temple" hairdo to compliment my outfit. In addition, I would receive a colorful Easter basket filled with assorted goodies. The night before Easter, we would boil plenty of eggs and color them for an egg hunt after church service. When church was out we would go to the park for a contest to see who could find the most eggs in an allotted amount of time. Whoever found the most eggs would win a prize, (as if the egg treasure was not prize enough).

It was a fun day. Laughter filled the air as our little feet ran swiftly to find the well-hidden eggs. Boy was I galvanized as I searched. I imagined that the eggs were treasures of whatever I wanted them to be. Before I knew it time had elapsed. I collected a few eggs but not enough to win the prize. But, what did I care? I'd just had a blast finding that which was once hidden.

Life is full of discovery. From my childhood memory to my adulthood actuality, I never stop finding things. Clues, signs, twist, and turns are everywhere pointing me to what I was designed to be. These objects of direction may not always be in "obvious" places, but certainly there are on the vivid scenes of life. Now of course I'm not looking for colored eggs anymore, I'm searching and capturing something that my very existence depends upon. It is not hiding from me, but I hide in it. It is—the living Word of God.

"My son, if you receive my words, and treasure my commands within you, so that you incline your ear to wisdom, and apply your heart to understanding; Yes, if you cry out for discernment, and lift up your voice for understanding, if you seek her as silver, and search for her as for hidden treasures; then you will understand the fear of the Lord, and find the knowledge of God" (Proverbs 2:1-5).

W W W. GOD

In the previous allegory concerning Mr. Will B. Dunn, every thing implies a deeper meaning. The gold he was dipped in represents: God's **W**ord, **W**ill, and **W**isdom which are simultaneously inclusive. These three are persistent in the Holy Bible, *"God's Autobiography"*, a gold mine within itself. [Italics mine].

In the natural, gold is a very precious metal. This metal has several qualities, which have made it exceptionally valuable throughout history. It is attractive in color and luster, its sleek appearance is eye catching. Gold is durable and it resists corrosion. This precious metal also serves as a means of exchange. Therefore, it is necessary that it be carefully and diligently guarded. But there is something that is esteemed and honored much more than even the finest gold-the Word of the Lord! The **W**ord of the Lord!

You see, the Word, is a treasure for a treasured people. It's filled with riches beyond compare. The radiant jewels of the Gospel of Jesus Christ, informs and transforms those who will repent and believe. The Spirit upon the holy writ is powerfully attractive and tastefully digestive. In fact, mans entire being can be sustained by it. No wonder Job said, *"I treasured thy word more than my necessary food"* (Job 23:12). All the Scriptures are masterfully given by Gods' own inspiration (see II Timothy 3:16). We have at our finger tips unlimited access to the prophetic Scriptures, foreseeing Scriptures, promising Scriptures, and Scriptures of comfort and hope. By virtue of this factual evidence alone, I'm assured that such a treasure of truth can be trusted.

In the Greek, the word inspiration is (*theopneustos*). Utilization of etymological application reveals that *Theo* which means God—plus *pneo* which means breath, equals— God breaths. Voila! Inspiration is defined.

In the human body breathing is connected to the respiratory system. The respiratory system is the exchange of carbon dioxide for oxygen via a function of (inhaling and exhaling) which occurs between an organism and its environment. Relative to the Living Word, Genesis 2:7 substantiates this belief as follows… Who in the beginning breathed life into man, and man became a living a soul. When man sinned against Him, God prepared Himself through His son Jesus, to come down from heaven, became flesh, and dwelt amongst us. (See John 1:14). He then reconnected us through the sacrificial system of redemption, buying us back with His own blood, and giving us access by the Eternal Spirit to operate the kingdom exchange in our lives (Eph 2:13,18). Since this exchange of the giving up the lesser for the greater transpired, God has empowered us to affect our environment. Through His Word, we know that He is closer than a prayer away; He's a sheer breath away!

Throughout the pages of the Bible are interesting details of the lives of chosen men and women who are called to participate in God's **W**ill. God has always implemented His plans through people. It is in the doing of His will for your life, that you experience the greatness of God. We must learn how to engage in that, which is already active in the will of God. The will of God is not at a stand still, but it is progressively in motion at all times.

What God had in store for His people—and the task laid before them—they could not afford to lean solely on their human intellect to get the job done. Instead, they had to lean on the Spirit of revelation to give them insight and guidance into His will.

Take note of Paul's candid prayer for the saints in Ephesus, after he heard of their faith in the Lord Jesus and love unto all the saints. It seems as though their commitment to follow Christ wholeheartedly qualified them for this prayer: *"That the God of our Lord Jesus Christ, the Father of glory, may give to you the spirit of wisdom and revelation in the knowledge of Him"* (Ephesians 1:17). Revelation connotes the disclosure of something unknown and giving it potential for becoming known… "That which man cannot find out for himself."

"O Lord, I know the way of man is not in himself; It is not in man who walks to direct his own steps (Jeremiah 10:23).

The Scripture above plainly indicates that it is not in man to order his own steps. Jesus said, *"…for without Me you can do nothing"* (John 15:5). Our own Noble Example didn't even order His own steps. When conversing with the Jews in John 5:19 *He {Jesus} answered and said unto them, "Most assuredly, I say to you, the Son can do nothing of Himself, but what He sees the Father do; for whatever He does, the Son also does in like manner."* Jesus walked continually by what the Father revealed unto Him.

It is pertinent for us to understand that the revelation of God is not "spooky" or inexplicable legendry that people must fear and dare to draw close to; neither is it only for the "elite" hero's of the Christian faith. Conversely, the spirit of revelation is an invitation leading to impartation, evoking the involvement of every Spirit-filled born again believer to go beyond the veil into the holy place where light is shed abroad. There you will see the Light of life giving knowledge and wisdom to any situation. As our eyes of understanding are being progressively opened, we behold excellent Truth that liberates us to do His perfect will. When we know our purpose in life—truth will motivate us to get things accomplished.

We are instructed by God through Apostle Peter to: … *"grow in grace and knowledge of our Lord and Savior Jesus Christ…"* (II Peter 3:18). When revelation springs forth from the Word, it comes to revitalize and reorganize our lives. Consequently, we must be flexible in doing what the Lord expresses through us. As we seek to stay involved in the will of God, we must be alert not allowing the natural man to dictate to us; because the natural man cannot receive the things of the Spirit of God. But, if the Spirit controls us, we can rely on Him to search and unveil the deep things of God. (See II Corinthians 2:10-14).

This same good Spirit that controls and leads us will also evoke within us a vital desire for **W**isdom to be our daily portion. For after something has been revealed, we then need wisdom to put it into effect.

The beauty and strength of wisdom is demonstrated in the life of Christ. Jesus was filled with wisdom—then He increased in wisdom—ultimately, He became the wisdom of God for us. All of His works are framed in wisdom.

The wisdom of God is unsearchable and boundless—yet reachable and practical. Life itself behooves us to welcome the wisdom of God. If wisdom is not welcomed, she can be misconstrued as a threat. Pride always opposes wisdom. Therefore, let us humbly comply by asking the Lord to *"teach us to number our days that we may gain a heart to wisdom"* (Psalms 90:12).

The character of wisdom embodies: listening, instruction, experience, skill, integrity, and the fear of the Lord. Notice that listening precedes the list and the fear of the Lord, its benediction. Everything else is nestled between the two. Now, *"the fear of the Lord is the beginning of wisdom"* (see Proverbs 9:10). How can it begin accept it be heard?

Listen, for I will speak of excellent things, and from the opening of my lips will come right things (Proverbs 8:6).

The above passage is wisdom giving audible instructions to listen. Robert Greenleaf stated: "From wisdom comes listening, from speaking comes repentance." It takes an inclined ear to hear wisdom cry aloud. If Jesus' ear was always engaged in covenant hearing to the Father's voice, shouldn't our ear be equally engaged as well? Hearing God nourishes our identity; our identity is well connected to revelation, which always leads to God's splendor being available to us.

The ear is one of the gates in which the way of wisdom enters. It consists of the external ear, the middle ear, and the inner ear. The inner ear is combined with the Vestibular System, which maintains balance and equilibrium in the body. To curtail this, it coordinates the cerebellum and the movements of the body to maintain it to the center of gravity. When the inner ear is infected, balance will waver. So, when your spiritual equilibrium becomes infected, it causes a spiritual imbalance.

"Wisdom and knowledge shall be the stability of your times…" (Isaiah 33:6). In this era in which we live, many things are continually vacillating. Values and convictions are on the rocks. The infection of sin is on the rampage and the only One who can pull us out of the mire is Jesus–the Solid Savior. He's the One "in whom all the treasures of wisdom and knowledge are hidden." (Colossians 2:3). If we will fall on our faces before Him and hearken sincerely, He will give stability in our lives and for our times. He will teach us how to stand and see the salvation of the Lord. Much can be said and learned about wisdom; after all she is before the ages of time. If you lack wisdom you can ask of God and it will be given when asked in faith. (See James 1:5). Wisdom is available for you and for your children's children. "The Lord stores up sound wisdom for the upright" (Proverbs 2:7).

If there ever was a man who was a lover of wisdom in the royalty of his time, history records that man was Solomon. When Solomon, King David's son, was set on the throne to rule, he asked God through a dream for an understanding heart in order to judge properly before God's people. His speech pleased the Lord and his request was granted in abundance. Right after wisdom entered his heart, he received opportunity to exercise it when a dilemma was presented to him. Two harlots came before the King and one said, *"This women and I dwell in the same house and I gave birth when she was in the house. Then it happened, the third day after I had given birth that this women also gave birth. And we were together and there was no one with us in the house. And this women's son died in the night, because she lay on him. So she arose in the middle of the night and took my son from my side, while your maidservant slept, and laid him in her bosom and laid her dead child in my bosom."* The account of the story goes on with one women's word against the other. But when the King had heard enough he commanded, *"Bring me a sword, divide the living child in two, and give half to one, and half to the other."* Then the women whose son was living spoke to the king, for she yearned with compassion for her son; and she said, *"O my lord, give her the living child, and by no means kill him!"* But the other said, *"Let him be neither mine nor yours, but divide him."* The king answered, *"Give the first women the living child, and by no means kill him; she is his mother"* (I Kings 3:9-28).

At first this story sounded pretty complicated to me until I saw wisdom come on the scene and save the day. That's the way wisdom works. It descends from above; surpasses perplexities; goes through and sees a way when there seems to be no way; brings success when failure is certain; and delivers glorious answers that dissolve pain and misfortune.

James 3:17 delineates the attributes characterizing godly wisdom. *"But the wisdom that is from above is first pure, then peaceable, gentle, willing to yield, full of mercy and good fruits, without partiality and without hypocrisy."* This scope of wisdom is evident in the story of King Solomon's decision resolving the "Babies' Mama Drama".

Let us also be lovers of the wisdom of God. God will allow both common and unusual situations to come where we are, so He can enable us to gain and exercise wisdom. She stands at the doorpost day and night waiting for us to request, receive, respond, and reign in wisdom. *"For wisdom is better than rubies, and all the things one may desire cannot be compared with her"* (Proverbs 8:11).

The treasure hunt is still on my friend. Dig deep into the unfolding of the Scriptures. We no longer have to be intimidated by what's hidden because our Lord through His **W**ord, **W**ill, and **W**isdom will bring it to the light. You still have time to pursue and find your riches in the secret place of God's heart.

CHAPTER SIX

Benefits in the Waiting

"Wait on the Lord; Be of good courage, and He shall strengthen
your heart; Wait, I say, on the Lord!"
Psalm 27:14

Most of us have heard the saying: "Patience is a virtue". Well, it most certainly is. Patience is a quality that can benefit anyone who will be trained by her. In case you thought it wasteful, know that waiting patiently on God is time well spent.

"Bless the Lord, O my soul and forget not all His benefits:" (Psalms 103:2)

In recalling the allegory, Mr. Will B. Dunn had to spend some time in the waiting room. He had just been taken out of the "boiling gold", only to find himself secluded in a corner on the wax paper. This paradox time for him, inconvenient yet needful, was beneficial to him so that he could repose on the prior events that took place. He probably questioned within, "What is really going on here?" I wonder if he gave consideration to the fact that patience had an integral part in defining the purpose of his transformation.

Wait In Hope

In the society in which we live there is so much haste and hustle that we neglect to take time to slow down and be still. We want things done fast, quickly, in a hurry, and now please! Instantaneousness seems to be the order of the day. Unfortunately, there is not a slot for God to fit into our "hurry box". His time is not in our hands. Thankfully, our times are in His hands. (Psalms 31:15)

I can recount various occasions when I have gone out and made blunders in my spending; drawn a misdirected conclusion over a situation; or moved ahead when I was supposed to standstill; stayed too long when I needed to make a move. The list goes on resulting in fiasco's that inspire lyrics like, "Get Me Out Jesus…Get Me Out Today"! Long after these diverse events when the dust had settled, I'd think to myself: "if only I had waited, things would have turned out differently." The fruit of patience encourages us to make better choices, and better choices yield a much sweeter reward. The wisdom of Solomon gave this perspective: *"Better is the end of a thing than the beginning thereof: and the patient in spirit is better than the proud in spirit"* (Ecclesiastes 7:8). KJV

I've observed while waiting for God to move in my life or give me the next piece of the puzzle, valuable lessons are being shared with me. One of the lessons shared is that I had to choose to wait in hope. In times past, I would slump into "feelings" of defeat when what I was waiting for didn't come through fast enough. I actually thought God would take pity on me and speed things up. Instead, He let me know that I was only hindering my faith and blocking the breakthrough that I needed. Finally, when I stopped trying to manipulate the circumstances to go my way and began praising God, trusting in His Word, that's when waiting in hope truly began.

When we wait in hope, the light and value of expectation blossoms in the manifested face of the miraculous. Don't allow the enemy to kill your expectation in God! Satan wants to drug you and I with the disappointments of life to numb the anticipation that God is going to do something awesome in our life as we actively wait on Him—He shall bring it to pass.

What other reason do we wrestle with waiting, besides "It's my blessing, and I want it now" attitude? Please don't misunderstand me, "now" is great—"Now faith is…" it is a position taken in confidence for the hope of the promise. But if rest and confidence are sifted out, what remains is fearful fretting. I believe that **one** of the reasons we wrestle with waiting is because waiting is sometimes associated with solitude. God has ordained specific times of solitude in our walk with Him to train our minds. The mind needs to be sound and settled so the Spirit can have interaction with it. This solitude period also teaches us how to reflect and be deeply rooted in the Word. When God allows this kind of beneficial solitude, He is teaching us something of Himself and calls for our undivided attention to observe His ways.

"I will instruct thee and teach thee in the way which thou shalt go: I will guide thee with mine eye." (Psalm 32:8) KJV

In order for God to lead us with His eye, we must develop a tender conscience toward Him by walking in the truth; pondering His word; and waiting on His counsel.

One of the ways He speaks is in a "still small voice". So, quiet yourself and listen. Don't be afraid of the solitude, but embrace it. For God is using this time to strengthen you internally.

With that in mind, patience must be experienced; for it is difficult to exercise anything for development in the "comfort zone". The writer of Hebrews 6:12 KJV affirms: *"That ye be not slothful, but followers of them who through faith and patience inherit the promises."* Many times we're concerned about the promise coming to pass, while God is concerned about our progress not being obstructed. Don't worry! God is trustworthy to perform His part.

Gleaning From the Life of Caleb

When I think about the need for patience being exercised and perseverance being developed in my life, the biblical character Caleb comes to mind. He comes to the "spotlight" of the Scriptures when being commissioned to investigate the land of Canaan. Out of twelve men representing each tribe, Caleb represents the tribe of Judah. (See Numbers 13:1-6).

Interestingly, we muse over the fact of how Abraham being a patriarch in the faith, waited twenty-five years for his promised seed. Abraham had to gird up the lions of his mind in the waiting because his faith was aimed at the fulfillment of the covenant. However, we cannot overlook Caleb, who "earnestly contended for the faith" waiting forty-five years for his inheritance. Talk about obedience and inspirational gumption—this Caleb fellow had it second to none!

Let's revisit what he communicates to Joshua, in Joshua 14:7-11,13

"I was forty years old when Moses the servant of the Lord sent me from Kadesh Barnea to spy out the land, and I brought back word to him as it was in my heart. Nevertheless my brethren who went up with me made the heart of the people melt, but I wholly followed the Lord my God. So Moses swore on that day, saying, "Surely the land where your foot has trodden shall be your inheritance and your children's forever, because you have wholly followed the Lord my God." And now behold, the Lord has kept me alive, as He said, these forty-five years, ever since the Lord spoke this word to Moses while Israel wandered in the wilderness; and now, here I am this day, eighty-five years old. As yet I am as strong this day as I was on the day that Moses sent me; just as my strength was then, so now is my strength for war, both for going out and for coming in."

"And Joshua blessed him, and gave Hebron to Caleb the son of Jephunneh as an inheritance."

What an incredible testimony! It apparently seems to me that Caleb set his determination according to what the Lord had spoken to him. He guarded that word and by it waged a good warfare. I could contemplate that every time he heard the Word of God through the lips of Moses, he submitted his mind to be renewed to it. He allowed the Word to be the **final authority** over his life and destiny. Caleb was not going to settle for less no matter what he had to endure or how long he had to wait. Focus and courage also came out of the Word spoken to him which was part of his daily ammunition; for he knew the Lord his God was keeping him alive and giving him strength to war, come in, and go out.

Even though Caleb was physically included in the years of wandering, he spiritually followed the Wonder of his salvation–Christ. Motivated by faith and vision, Caleb remained fruitful in a barren land giving God the praise. (See Number Chapter 13:30-33, Chapter 14:6-9, and 14:24). I want to underscore three concise points that pertain to his character, which appealed to me:

A. He took responsibility to calm down the people who were in an uproar over a bad report. The negative report brought back by the ten spies shook the people from the diminutive belief they did have, to fear and confusion (see Numbers 13:30). **What** the ten spies saw was true; there were giants in the land, but **how** they saw was false. They didn't see God with them; so consequently, the way they saw themselves had massively depreciated which in turn disabled them to fulfill what God wanted. Caleb, on the other hand was dressed in optimism. He went against the unbelieving grain, seeing what others couldn't see, and later received a harvest of blessing. In my assessment of Caleb, I see through the Scriptures that Caleb didn't see crystal clear in his own rational as to what was happening; after all, the wilderness was no "cake walk", but Caleb saw **glory clear** not relying on the things temporally seen. His inner assurance outweighed the opposition, thus giving him the boldness to speak about their ability to overcome.

B. Caleb along with Joshua instructed the people not to rebel against the Lord. They confirmed that the land was good and assured them of the Lord's faithfulness to be with them. (Numbers 14:6-9). I believe that Caleb knew he had the victory and engaged himself in that victory by refusing to complain. When we yield to the way of complaining, it leads to the contamination of spirit, but Caleb had a **"different spirit."** Caleb had insurmountable circumstances with the children of Israel to overcome and he could have fell prey to the cynicism and forfeited the promise. Caleb's experience with God set him apart as an example, which authorized him to instruct the people to believe rather than rebel. *"For* *rebellion is as the sin of witchcraft, and stubbornness is as iniquity and idolatry….* (I Samuel 15:23a)

C. Caleb, the servant of the Lord, maintained his steadfastness by having a different spirit in him.

He completely followed the Lord, while having a challenge positioned before him and a doubtful people encompassed about him (see Numbers 14:24). Caleb beheld the glory of the Lord and internalized it. The glory of the Lord refreshed his existence on a daily basis. The glory of the Lord transported him to his victorious inheritance. According to Numbers 13:22, other men saw the glory and the signs too, but it is evident that they didn't appreciate it or heed to the voice of the Lord.

Because of the sobering gear of creative persistence, Caleb's dedication to the process rewarded him, taking him from glory to glory. *"Now, the Lord is the Spirit; and where the Spirit of the Lord is, there is liberty"* (II Corinthians 3:17). Caleb had the Spirit of his Father, the Lord. He pressed undauntedly forward, because he valued the Word and works of God. He desired for his brothers to crossover with him, but if they refused to comply, he was not going to allow **anyone to disqualify him.**

Today, these same points can be applied to our lives as we patiently wait upon the Lord.

First, if you don't have a people to calm down, calm yourself down.

> *"Lord, my heart is not haughty, nor my eyes lofty. Neither do I concern myself with great matters, nor with things too profound for me. Surely I have calmed and quieted my soul, like a weaned child with is mother; like a weaned child is my soul within me"* (Psalm 131:1-2).

With so much around us vying for our attention–family, business, physical challenges, financial pressures, trials, etc.–we must seek refuge under the wings of our loving Father. We learn how to come again and again to an inward surrender, letting God be God in every situation. In the Word of God we have a hiding place. No matter what report comes our way, we definitively can believe and trust in the report of the Lord.

It's amazing how fresh insight from the Holy Scriptures will stimulate your mind and bring a calming tranquility. Allow God's powerful peace to guard your heart. During this time we can quiet ourselves and have rule over our own spirit. (Proverbs 16:32).

"For thus says the Lord God, the Holy One of Israel: In returning and rest you shall be saved; in quietness and confidence shall be your strength…" (Isaiah 30:15).

Secondly, remind yourself not to rebel against the Lord.

We should daily put off the old man with his deeds; put on the whole armor of God; and put on the new man. (See Colossians 3:9-10, Ephesians 6:11,). The carnal cannot relate to the Spirit because the carnal mind/behavior is rebellious to the life of faith. Only one of the two, the Spirit or the flesh will dominate our heart. Rebellion causes you to lose ground, and leaves you dwelling in a dry land, cursed, and without production. Let us prayerfully acknowledge and identify any areas of rebellion and repent.

However, the antithesis of rebellion is obedience. Obedience secures victory and pleases God because it flourishes out of faith. It may not always be easy but His grace will be supplied for us to fulfill what He requires of us. In obeying the Word of the Lord, your determination will be met with opposition, but don't let it deter you! "Happy are they who trust and obey."

"If you are willing and obedient, you shall eat the good of the land; But if you refuse and rebel, you shall be devoured by the sword; For the mouth of the Lord has spoken" (Isaiah 1:19-20).

Finally, continue to be steadfast in the faith cultivating good works.

Have you found yourself going through the motions of service, feeling indifferent towards your mission? My word to you is, **"Don't lose heart!** Keep doing what is right and good. You have to ask yourself whether you're simply looking for a returned favor, or are you looking for your harvest?" There is a fresh wind—a fresh revival of God's presence coming your way if you faint not. Press into the glory of God and allow the glory to enlarge your capacity and competence. When we submit our heart and our works to Christ, we allow the reign of His authority to bond us to unbroken steadfastness in Him.

Good works were ordained for us to walk in; and they are stirred by employing the Word to our hearts. When we are engaged in doing good works, having a grateful heart will inspire us not to take things for granted; it will also help us to watch our attitude towards our assignments. We too can have a "different spirit" by walking in the Spirit and praising God. Keep on reaching for growth and development, for soon you will experience the harvest of your labor in the Lord. Connect with people who are doing good, who want to see you do good.

"This is a faithful saying, and these things I want you to affirm constantly, that those who have believed in God should be careful to maintain good works. These things are good and profitable to men" (Titus 3:8).

Weeds that Hinder the Benefits

Patience is not only a virtue it also serves as a part of Gods' protection for our lives. It introduces times and seasons which are predetermined by God's wisdom. Without these in place, mass befuddlement would run rampant leaving us frustrated and bent on a path to self-destruction. Even though God is not governed by time because He is eternal, He uses time and seasons for His purpose and has allotted time for mans' use.

Since the spirit of patience can assist to shield us from subtle dangers, we must also be alert of negative influences that come to counter-act patience. Some of these influences are: **Anxiety, Weariness,** and **Discouragement.**

Hebrews 12:1 declares, *"Therefore we also, since we are surrounded by so great a cloud of witnesses, let us lay aside every weight, and the sin which se easily ensnares us, and let us run with endurance the race that is set before us,.."*

These deterrents are like weeds that keep us preoccupied with fearful thoughts. They snatch our mental energies away, and provoke high-leveled stress. These deadly weeds come to deprive courage and confidence, causing a slow drain of the emotions accompanied by a downward pull into deep depression. You may feel like giving up because you can't take it any longer. The act of perseverance can become like an annoying burden when weariness tags along.

"Then they journeyed from mount Hor by the way of the Red Sea, to go around the land of E-dom: and the soul of the people was much discouraged because of the way" (Numbers 21:4 KJV).

We have all had encounters with discouragement. It comes in the major and minor melodies of everyday life. If we succumb and waddle in discouragement, it will systematically weaken us until we spiritually fade away. God has given us everlasting encouragement even in the midst of the storm. We can be in the storm, or around the storm, but don't allow the storm to get in you!

These weeds that come to encroach upon us must be combated with the Word of God. You can also speak healing words to yourself; surround yourself with people who are weil grounded in the faith; change up a mundane routine; and let the joy of the Lord be your strength. (See Nehemiah 8:10). If you happen to find yourself in one or all three categories of being anxious, wearied, or discouraged, remember the words of the Lord Jesus when He spoke: *"Come to Me, all you who labor and are heavy laden, and I will give you rest. Take My yoke upon you and learn from Me, for I am gentle and lowly in heart, and you will find rest for your souls. For my yoke is easy and My burden is light"* (Matthew 11:28-30).

The Benefit Package

They're many blessings the Lord has prepared for us to receive. The enemy is angry and tries to initiate a level of warfare behind the blessing; but there is nothing he can do to stop Gods' people from being blessed. Everyone may not be happy for you as they witness the goodness of God being bestowed upon you. Your success may be perceived as an intimidating threat or rejection by those who think you will forget about them or act indifferent towards them. In such cases as this, the Lord will prepare us.

"Look unto Abraham your father, and unto Sarah that bare you: for I called him alone, and blessed him and increased him" (Isaiah 51:2, KJV).

Our blessings are never designed to belittle anyone, but they are designed to build and to bless others for the glory of God. Humility is conducive to the blessings of God; therefore, we cannot afford to shred the integrity of our blessings by trying to prove to people that we will not change. The **"I told you so"** attitude toward those who thought we would never make, is equally deleterious. We must all bear in mind that privilege and sensitivity also come with the blessings from above.

After you've suffered, survived your experiences, and are right now still living life by faith, these are a few sampling of the innumerable benefits that will be made manifest unto you and I:

(Deuteronomy 28:2) The blessings of God will come and overtake you.
(Psalm 37:9) We will inherit the earth.
(Job 14:14) A change will be come soon.
(Psalm 27:14) Be of good courage. God will strengthen your heart.
(Psalm 62:5) Expectations in and of God will not be disappointed.
(Psalm 145:15) He will give us meat in due season.

(Isaiah 40:31) Strength is renewed to mount up with wings like eagles, run and not be weary, walk and not faint.

(Habakkuk 2:3) What God has promised it will surely come to pass.

(James 5:7/Luke 8:15) Precious fruit will be produced and increased.

(Psalm 34:10) They that seek the Lord will not lack any good thing.

(Psalm 16:6) The lines will fall to you in pleasant places; absolutely, you have a good inheritance.

Wow! What an awesome benefit package that God has uniquely established for those who wait on Him. **See if you can find some more in your study time.**

There is some left over gold that has trickled down from your experiences. Others' will come behind and anticipate the wisdom gained from our period of testing. Therefore, I encourage you to lavishly share what God has done for you. Tell how He can recycle your pain into purpose with His transforming grace. Don't delay, because this generation is waiting–waiting for the benefits.

CHAPTER SEVEN

In the Heat but Not Without Hope

"But who may abide the day of his coming? And who shall stand when he appeareth?
For he is like a refiner's fire, and like a fullers soap: And he shall sit as a refiner
and purifier of silver: and he shall purify the sons of Levi, and purge them as gold
and silver, that they may offer unto the Lord an offering in righteousness."
Malachi 3:2–3

There is an old motto that states: **"If you can't stand the heat, get out of the kitchen"**… but in the Kingdom of God, that statement is obsolete! According to *Webster's New World Dictionary*, Second College Edition—the word **fire** is defined as: "any preparation that will burn and make a brilliant display; or extreme distress that tries one's endurance." "God is a consuming fire" (Hebrews 12:29 KJV). The Bible also declares that God "has chosen us in the furnace of affliction" (Isaiah 49:10 KJV). He specializes in turning weakness into strength, frustrations into foresight, making rough places smooth, crooked places straight and turning opposition into opportunity through His exquisite grace. The mysterious art of this transforming work often takes place in the midst of the fire. Trying to escape it or embarking upon a career as a fire fighter is futile.

All this boils down to one word: **suffering!** I know, just what you wanted to hear, right? The Apostle Paul said, *"For unto you it is given in the behalf of Christ, not only to believe on him, but also to suffer for his sake"* (Philippians 1:29 KJV). Most of us have the believing part down (or do we?), but suffering for His sake is another story altogether. Nobody enjoys facing the fires of life. I cannot find too many people who volunteer their spare time for heartache and sorrow. Nevertheless, the truth remains that "all who desire to live godly in Christ Jesus shall suffer persecution" (II Timothy 3:12). So we might as well let these "light afflictions" work for us and bring us into the refined state that the Father counsels us to live in.

I have found through observation mostly of my own life, that suffering, weather it be physical, mental, or spiritual, can serve as a footstool. A footstool helps to lift one up in order to reach that which they couldn't reach before. Suffering works the same way through faith by helping us reach levels in Christ that we could not get to on our own. Suffering is not an end in itself; it only aids to shape us on the pathway to Christlikeness if we allow it to. In his book, *"Don't Waste Your Sorrows"*, Paul Bullheimer beautifully conveys: **"All affliction is intended to drive one to God. It is intended to work a fuller submission, a more utter devotion, an increasing patience, a greater beauty of spirit, a more selfless love toward both God and man. When it accomplishes this, then it may be classified as suffering *with* Christ and for His sake because it has enabled Him to achieve His end and purpose in that one."**

When I earnestly seek God for who He is, a consuming hunger and thirst for the more of His presence and anointing surges in me. But while I yearn for Him, at times, He allows the strong winds of adversity to come and assist me into higher realms. We don't always recognize this at first, but in time the purpose of that particular trial will be revealed. In looking at the life of Jesus, we find that He would not return to the place of His Father in glory, except He drink of the cup of suffering. It was His fulfilled obedience and suffering that "transmitted" Him back to heaven. He could have called a legion of angels to come and get Him, but instead He yielded His soul to the Father's will.

> *"Confirming the souls of the disciples, and exhorting them to continue in the faith, and that **we must through much tribulation enter in to the kingdom of God"** (Acts 14:22 KJV). {Emphasis added}.*

What's in You Will Come Out

The fires of life are not meant to destroy you, but to make a brilliant display of God's glory in your life. The Faithful Accountant has invested much through the stock of His Servant, Jesus, and He wants multiplied back what He has put in.

> *"For it is God who works in you both to will and to do for His good pleasure"* (Philippians 2:13).

As I reflect back on my beautiful mother Gladys, a godly woman, and an awesome cook would often make delicious pound cakes that would melt in your mouth and make you pat your feet. I can recall sitting at the kitchen counter watching her gather the ingredients, mixing them in a bowl, then pouring it into a cake pan, and placing the cake pan into a preheated oven. I waited with anticipation while looking through the glass oven window as the liquid batter was metamorphosing, turning into a delicious cake. Everything my mother put into the cake produced her desired intentions. In other words, what she put in—came out.

> *"But he knoweth the way that I take: When he hath tried me, I shall come forth as gold* (Job 23:10 KJV).

Notice that Job didn't say, "he is making me like gold," but "**I shall come forth as gold**." {Emphasis added}. This is an indication that Job already had in him the righteous "ingredients" of the Lord. However, fire was the famous force that purged and pulled the "gold" out. Reviewing Job's relationship with God prior to the catastrophic events in his life solidifies this fact. You see, we will produce only what we conceive, weather it be positive or negative. The seed of the Word must be conceived in our spirit not our emotions to produce life.

Job was a man that esteemed God's Word and held fast to His steps. (See Job 23:11:12). His intimacy with God, coupled with the fear of the Lord produced in him an inner might that cleaved unto the Lord in devastating times. His worship "branded" him from the very start. Job was not only a favored man; he was a found man because he "worshiped in spirit and in truth".

> *"And the Lord said unto Satan, Hast thou considered my servant Job, that there is none like him in the earth, a perfect and an upright man, one that feareth God, and escheweth evil? And still he holdeth fast his integrity, although thou movedst me against him, to destroy him without cause"* (Job 2:3 KJV).

Out of all that Job went through, it's important to understand that God never changed His mind about him. God's Word is irrevocable no matter what Satan tries to do. Although, Job's troubles did affect him, they did not eliminate him. Satan couldn't destroy Job because the Word had been put in him and spoken over him. That Word also lifted up a standard against the plot of the enemy. Satan will come to tempt us on every turn as well (he must receive permission from God), but the Helper will come, making a way of escape for us.

Fire, interestingly, will expose any foible and purge impurities that will tarnish the vessels. It is of necessity that we have an acute awareness of our inner life and inner thoughts, because "character does count". Character is to be founded upon

Gods' truth and must be developed as we learn. It is far more than information received, character is the **quality** of life expressed. The author of Hebrews 5:8 penned: *"Though he were a Son, yet **learned he obedience** by the things which he suffered."* Paul records in Philippians 2:8, *"And being found in appearance as a man He humbled Himself and **became obedient** to the point of death, even the death of the cross."* {Emphasis added}. Jesus, in His humanity learned and became obedient. He always exemplified the quality of life because He always pleased the Father (see John 8:29).

Character reveals the hidden man of the heart, and this is why we are prompted to "guard our heart with all diligence; for out it are the issues of life" (Proverbs 4:23). God can use us at anytime but if we want Him to advance us, refined character is required. One of His desires for us is to pass the test until He sees Himself.

> *"Each one's work will become clear; for the Day will declare it, because it will be revealed by fire; and the fire will test each one's work, of what sort it is. tested by fire to see what sort it is"* (I Corinthians 3:13).

Therefore, we must build upon the solid foundation of Jesus Christ that our works may endure through the fire. Character development is a continual process, it doesn't take place over night. Please let us be patient with one another keeping in mind that God is not through with us yet.

Walking Through the Flames

I remember a time in my life when there was anguish and trauma. I was married but my relationship was on a rocky road, not knowing if we would make it or not. I was in my early twenties and selfishly had my own version of an "ideal marriage" in mind. Unfortunately, this just wasn't cutting it. I had my faults and my mistakes, renamed as we "live and we learn". As time went on in my marriage, I found out that I was pregnant with our first child. At first I wasn't too happy about that either because of the situation, but I came to embrace and love my unborn child, waiting for her arrival.

One night I had a dream that I was going to have a little girl; her name was to be Lydia Deborah Queen (I added Queen). The pregnancy went smooth. Every time I went to the doctor, the baby's heartbeat was strong; we were both in good standing. A friend hosted for me wonderful Baby Shower with lots of nice gifts; I remember the fellowship being cordially fun.

Early one Sunday morning in June, I awakened to fix some breakfast and set out to have a relaxing day, I was in my ninth month of pregnancy. Later on in the day I felt weak and had the chills so I lay down for a while and got back up that evening. A few minutes after I got up, my water broke and I told my husband, "It's that time. Here comes the baby"!

When I arrived at the hospital they took care of the normal procedures then checked for the baby's heartbeat, but couldn't find it. They checked three times and on the third time there was a strong heartbeat that I could hear. I told the nurse, "There it is! Her heartbeat is always very strong." The nurse replied, "Ma'am, that's your heartbeat. We are sorry to inform you that your baby is dead." I was devastated and in disbelief at what my ears had just heard. I thought to my self, "Well, if she is dead, surely the Lord will raise her up!" But He didn't! I ended up having to go through 20 hours of the entire birthing process and delivered a pretty nine pound still born baby girl. Silently, she passed away in my womb because the umbilical cord strangled her.

There seemed to be no reasonable explanation in my mind of why this thing had happened–happened to me! I recall asking my sister-in-law after labor, "What did God say about it?" It was a time of great perplexity. I felt the fire all around me but thank God, I didn't burn up! The silence of this predicament simmered in the heat, while it seemed as if God was not around. Someone brought me a journal while I was still in the hospital to jot down my thoughts. I would like to candidly share some of what I wrote:

June 5th Wednesday afternoon:

"Here I am laying in this hospital trying to rest and find some peace over the loss of my baby Lydia. It seems like I'm working through a million-piece puzzle trying to put it together, yet not really knowing where to start. So much pain and hurt that I'm acquainted with right now. Understanding is out of my reach and my womb has been emptied out. I wish my life had been taken instead of hers, not in a bad sense, but because of the sacrifice. I long to hear her sweet voice cry–I wanted to say to her, "Welcome" instead of "Good by".

The labor was intense. However, I know that I did the best I could though it still feels like I've failed. What a blow to my heart! It feels like the wind has been knocked out of me! I feel like I've been robbed with no way of recovering my baby girl back. I would have never suspected this, even though I know that things are going to happen to me in life and I must go on.

Someone asked me a question the other day: "Charlene, how do you feel about God now?" I replied, "I choose to worship Him. I don't want to be bitter towards Him. What good would that do anyhow?" I must keep seeking His face even though the enemy is wrestling with my mind about God's love for me. I know the Lord loves and cares for me in the midst of it all. I can still see His hand on my life. It is He who is holding the reins of mind right now. I'm sure the enemy would have liked to destroy me through this, but I'm a survivor through Christ Jesus."

*(Later I wrote these words): "I believe that one purpose of Lydia's short lived life was to bring me to a more committed life in my service to God. And to follow after God no matter what may happen. No time to give up! When trials and pain come like now, I often think of the dream I had concerning the man who was tried in the fire, "**Coming Forth as Gold.**"*

I was out of the hospital now and recuperating at home, when one morning I heard the Holy Spirit's voice say, "Charlene, rejoice! This was done in love." That sentence ministered hope to me because it let me know that I was not being punished for something I had done; neither was God lashing out His anger at me. I needed to know that I was loved and still wanted by God. I was weak, but my faith in the Scripture came alive, the Scripture of comfort that states: "Who shall separate us from the love of Christ? (Romans 8:35a) I may never know the full reason why this happened, but I had to trust His character. "God is love".

Seven months later, (January) I was divorced and during this time my mother was in a battle with breast cancer. The cancer went into remission for about a year in a half but it came back with such an aggression. I remember going to the doctor with her for the last time, he told her they had done all that they could do. He said that she had around six months to live but she died in three months, (March) gone to be with the Lord. She passed two days before my twenty-seventh birthday.

All this happened to me within a ten-month time frame, yet God was holding me together. The heat was pretty intense but the Hope of Glory saw me through. There were times when I thought I was not going to make it; times when I was numb to the pain but that served as a shield for God to complete the surgery in my heart. The mercy of God knew the set timing that I was to come out, and after a while I could hear in the Spirit the "beeper" going off.

Like the dross surfacing to the top of the gold to be scrapped off, so was I in like manner. I had a choice in reaction to these trials, either I was going to be bitter or get better. I embraced the better. I sought the Lord much during this time, inquiring about a lot of things, and receiving the truth that set me free. I took one day at a time as I walked with my hand in His; He became my Beloved Therapist on the healing journey. For grace had explored the damage done and brought it the High Priest our Healing Balm, and the High Priest looked at it and declared: **"I Am the Lord that heals you, I care for you."** Praise be to the God of my life!

Riding on the Wings of Faith

Sometimes, God needs to tear up in order to set us up for a miraculous blessing. Job said it like this, *"I was at ease, but he hath broken me asunder; he has also taken me by my neck, and shaken me to pieces, and set me up for his mark"* (Job 16:12 KJV). No matter what may be torn up in your life right now, keep in mind that the battle is temporary but who you're to become in Christ is permanent. God has something set-aside just for you. The fire has branded the blessing with an authenticity that the devil cannot duplicate or destroy. Apostle Peter gave the saints hopeful insight concerning their trials saying: *"In this you greatly rejoice, though now for a little while, if need be, you have been grieved by various trials, that the genuineness of your faith, being much more precious than gold that perishes, though it is tested by fire, may be found to praise, honor, and glory at the revelation of Jesus Christ"* (I Peter 1:6-7). We want to receive the results of a found faith–found unto praise, honor and glory. It is our faith that is under attack. The enemy will fight what you live by concerning righteousness. Why? Because the "just shall **live by** faith" and **"without faith** it is impossible to please God." It is with the **shield of faith** that we will be able to "quench all the fiery darts of the wicked one". (See Romans 1:17, Hebrews 11:6 and Ephesians 6:16). {Emphasis added}.

Faith keeps hope alive in our heart while facing the fire. Faith will never lead us down a dead end street, but will create a way for us to pass through. Living by the faith of God will bear you up and bring you safely to the haven of your destiny. By faith God is still able to deliver His people out of the furnace today. Hope still abounds for you. Shake off the ashes of unbelief and ascend in His presence.

> *"And thou shalt be secure, because there is hope; yea, thou shalt dig about thee, and thou shalt take thou rest in safety"* (Job 11:18 KJV).

Whoever is reading this, I say to you in the midst of the fire, **"Hold on! The "beeper" is about to go off."** You will come out without the smell of smoke–you will not be burned! The fire is going to bring you through the survival mode into a continual nourishing place of security. Jesus is in there with you; He is speaking to you right in the heat of your situation. Hear His anointed voice echo throughout your being, **I LOVE YOU**! The fan is in His hand and He won't let it get out of control. After a while, you will come out shining like gold reflecting the Father's heart. Now get ready for a new refreshing start.

CHAPTER EIGHT

The Pool: Refreshing Times Are Here Again!

"Repent therefore and be converted that your sins may be blotted out, so that times of refreshing may come from the presence of the Lord".
Acts 3:19

My soul is parched—yet my soul looks up, because I hear the beautiful flowing sound of the water falls whirling around me. "O devoted waters of life fall on me! Fill my cup while I rejoice in the One who has provided an oasis in the desert for me." There is a cooling time—a time to be refreshed from the fires of life. There is a place of rest, which our faith brings us into because we have dared to hold on.

When you are in the heat for a durable time, your strength is be depleted, you're in need of replenishing. David in his passion verbalizes: *"As the hart panteth after the water brooks, so panteth my soul after thee, O God. My soul thirsteth for God, for the living God: when shall I come and appear before God?"* (Psalm 42:1-2 KJV). As we thirst for the water, the Divine Shepherd leads His flock beside still pure waters that run deep and smooth. The Shepherd knows that it is difficult for sheep to drink freely from raging waters.

Come, and sit in the pool my brothers and sisters. Allow Him to wash you with the "washing of water by the word"… (Ephesians 5:26). Go ahead, give yourself the permission to feel the bubbling water and the gentle breeze that surrounds you. Blessed tranquillity enfolds us as we unwind from the pressures of the heat and take the opportunity to give thanks unto the Lord. As you make contact with the waters there will be a thick vapor, (His glory) that will appear and fill the atmosphere with a charge that cannot be denied. Everyone will know by your lighted countenance that you have been invigorated in the presence of Jesus.

Charlene Gardner

What Did You Learn?

"As in water face answereth to face, so the heart of man to man" (Proverbs 27:19 KJV).

While basking in the water we reflect on the time when we were in the heat of the fire, and we learned certain peculiarities about ourselves that were not readily known before. Sinful matters of the heart were brought to light as the candle of the Lord blazed within. The fire burned past the surface into the very root of our being. I learned that the surface isn't always safe, but that the "name of the Lord is a strong tower; the righteous run to it and they are safe" (Proverbs 18:10). Our experience in the fire has caused us to confront those issues that we have tried to hide or ignore for so long.

Let me ease your heart a little by saying, confrontation doesn't have to be a dread; it can actually be constructive in many cases. Confrontation coupled with wisdom may help remove some of the obstructions that have delayed our growth. But on the other hand, **unhealthy** denial is an assassin to true peace. It ensnares your mind and emotions with your eyes wide open because there is a **willingness** that exists to close the "acknowledgement valve" to your heart. Living in denial keeps you unprepared for the next thing that is about to happen because it lurks in the shadows of darkness attempting to suppress the truth; the truth is always there, and eventually the truth will prevail. This alerts us to why some people don't receive inward healing even after their trouble. If we simply, yet courageously take an inner look, then inner healing can begin. What we must constantly realize is that God already knows all about us. He knows us better than we know ourselves and He loves us. It's all right to be transparent in His presence. He's the One that created you and me. He desires for us to be completely honest with Him. He wants us to allow Him to get to the root of the matter because–He is the Root!

The Word declares, *"Behold, You desire truth in the inward parts, and in the hidden part You will make me to know wisdom"* (Psalm 51:6).

Another aspect of this special time is getting to see what still remains. There is still something creative, exceptional, loving, and attractive that you have to offer. **Better** is on the menu and its taste is mouth-wateringly delicious. Since there is healing in the revealing as we accept the truth, it will not only set us free, but it will speed up our spiritual metabolism in order to bring closure to situations and move on. It's motivating to know that absolute truth is available to us every 24 hours, 7 days a week, 365 days a year, in every season, and on every level. Truth is unchangeable! Jesus Christ is Truth! Therefore, hope is always abounding for us as we open our hearts to it.

True Repentance: The Way to Renewal

While we walk in the path of this Christian journey and the besetting sins are unmasked, we should repent quickly which denotes a change and conviction of the heart and mind. We need a change in our will to live God's way and a conviction not to regress into bondage. Thus, true repentance enables us to walk in agreement with God and have "fruit unto holiness". True repentance revives our heart to the reality of the kingdom of God. It restores intimacy and impels us into covenant relationship with the Father which in turn establishes deeper trust and unity. God wants us to return back to Him with our whole hearts setting our affections on our "first love", Jesus Christ. God must be our priority in life and ministry. He will not tolerate His people putting Him on the back burner, acting indifferent, while they conduct business as usual! Even now, some are walking in an unrepentant state and are oblivious to kingdom principals; they go to church but are alienated by iniquitous works. Jesus repeatedly knocks on the door of many hearts that were once tuned in with Him. Think about it, the Door knocking at the door! But religion and the traditions of men have hung out the **"Do Not Disturb"** sign, which keeps Christ at bay. They want what He has to offer but are not willing to get intimately acquainted with Him. As a result, desensitization of the conscience towards confession and repentance has left their hearts undone. Some people are doing the "work" of the Lord but their relationship with Him has dropped off. We must remember that the Father is seeking for those who will "worship Him in spirit and truth" (see John 4:23-24).

Gehazi, Rocks the Boat

Gehazi, a servant to Prophet Elisha in the Old Testament, was an example of this lukewarm state that some in the church have fallen prey to in this hour. His tragic end begins in the biblical account of II Kings Chapter Five. The narrative opens with Naaman, who is a commander of the army of the king of Syria, a great and honorable man. Ironically, even though he was great, he was a leper. Obviously, he desires to be healed from his leprosy condition and one day hears a word from his wife's mistress saying, *"If only my master were with the prophet who is in Samaria! For he would heal him of his leprosy."* A letter is sent to the king of Israel, advising that he would heal Naaman from his leprosy. When the king read the letter, he tore his clothes, saying, *"Am I God, to kill and make alive, that this man sends a man to me to heal him of his leprosy?" When Elisha, the man of God heard the king had torn his clothes,* he inquired about the situation. Elisha stated, *"Please let him come to me." And he sent a messenger to him saying, "Go and wash in the Jordan seven times, and you flesh will be restored to you and you will be clean."* But Naaman acted acrimonious towards the command and wanted to wash in another river. One of Naaman's servants came near him and spoke wisdom—he heeded, and dipped in the Jordan seven times. His flesh was then restored like the flesh of a little child. Then he came to Elisha and stood before him, he also acknowledged that there is no God in all the earth, except in Israel. Naaman is grateful and would like to show it by giving a gift. However, the man of God will not accept it whatsoever. But Gehazi, the servant of Elisha, has a different frame of mind saying to himself, *"Look, my master, has spared Naaman this Syrian, while not receiving from his hands what he brought; but as the Lord lives, I will run after him and take something from him."* So Gehazi pursued Naaman. He lied to Naaman, saying, *"My master sent me, and two young prophets have come from the mountains of Ephraim. Please give them a talent of silver and two changes of garments."* Being in a generous mood, Naaman gives Gehazi a double portion of what he asks. *"Now he went and stood before Elisha, and Elisha said to him, "Where did you go, Gehazi?" And he said, "Your servant didn't go anywhere." Then he said to him, "Did not my heart go with you when the man turned back from his chariot to meet you? Is it time to receive money and to receive clothing, olive groves, and vineyards, sheep and oxen, male and female servants? Therefore the leprosy of Naaman shall cling to you and your descendants forever."* *"And he went out from his presence leprous, as white as snow."*

It's intriguing to know that Gehazi's name means: ***"valley of a visionary; to gaze at; to mentally perceive (with pleasure)."*** Gehazi had many wonderful opportunities. He constantly was working with a noble and powerful prophet assisting him in the work of the Lord. He saw many miracles; stood in awe of the power of God, but did not allow the glory of God to apprehend or penetrate his heart. What happened to him? **He was supposed to carry on the vision with the pleasure of God on his life.** He was supposed to move forward in the mantle, the mission and the demand of the prophetic. Was he just going for the ride without understanding kingdom priorities? Was he tired of seeing others get blessed, while what he desired got put on the back shelf? Was serving others starting to get on his nerves? Did this impulsive act to go back to Naaman arise due to "insufficient funds" during his "God will make a way" journey? Or was there something furtive circulating in his heart little by little. May I **suggest** that greed and selfish ambition was the downfall of this potential carrier of the anointed mantle. Gehazi's untimely pursuit of material things forfeited the double portion that he was to receive and because of his disobedience, he and his descendants contracted leprosy forever. All that time in his "master's" presence and yet he didn't seem to realize that Elisha's **heart** was with him every where he went. With every move of God, the Spirit is consistently trying to draw us closer in the ways of God.

In this dispensation of grace that we live in now, it is imperative that we don't receive "this grace in vain". The Lord is the Spirit that searches our heart and is with us every step of the way. Don't be deceived! We are more accountable to God than we've ever been before. Trying to be empowered without taking inventory of our life is hazardous! Let us consider our ways and mend them now while the blood is still running warm in our veins. Let us monitor our hearts diligently. He wants to rain upon us and renew us afresh with love blooming in hearts until the day of His return.

Restoration is in the House

This is the hour of restoration for the body of Christ. Even though the locust, cankerworm, caterpillar, and the palmerworm have eaten up some years, God is willing to restore your harvest (see Joel 2:25-26). I know the enemy has shouted some doubtful suggestions that perhaps: "God has changed His mind about you. Or that it's too late in day for your promise to be fulfilled". **But the devil is a liar**! You may have felt at times that you were going to slip away without any solutions to your problems. But Jesus, the Resurrection, has come to restore all things unto Himself.

You see restoration was ordained for us. It is a spiritual blessing that we have been blessed with. God spoke it through the mouth of His holy prophets since the world began. (See Acts 3:21). It was hidden in Christ Jesus and since we are hid in Christ, through the blood of His covenant, we can abide in a place of restoration. All we need to do is receive it by faith right now!

Jesus is sending the balm of His restoring power to those areas where you may have had a loss of someone or something in your life; He knows how to fill the void. There may be some whose fellowship might be broken with the saints and you've stopped going to the house of the Lord and have become like "sheep without a shepherd". You may be saying, "Well, sister, I was wounded in the church that's why I don't go anymore." But there is a restoring word to the wounded. The Lord says, *"For I will restore health to you and heal you of your wounds, because they called you an outcast saying: This is Zion; No one seeks her"* (Jeremiah 30:17). Listen, as He compassionately calls you out by name to come back into the fold and be joined unto Him. Please, do away with the estrangement in your heart towards Him. You lost your focus, putting your eyes on man. You saw some "off-the-wall" behavior and allowed it to push you away. Grievously, many have inflicted ill treatment, ill words, and underhandedness in the body of Christ. You were met with some strong resistance, but God wants to meet you on the mountain with sweet surprises of His love! **Alleluia**! Due to pride, I'm sorry to inform you that many won't be getting a personal apology. Yet, with the help of the Holy Spirit, you can overcome! It's important to believe in the body of Christ that "the Lord will perfect that which concerns me" (Psalm 138:8). We must walk in love. With His loving-kindness, He longs to put you back in place. You cannot afford to miss out on the next dimension that God has for His beloved ones.

Come on in the House, It's Going to Rain!

God is getting His house ready for the glorious outpour of His Spirit. His church, "the called out ones" will not just have "a revival" but the Spirit of revival shall rest upon the people. God is purifying His house, breathing fresh order upon it; and clothing it with beauty. He is also teaching and preparing His people through the Word how to flow in the rivers of the Spirit. They're are willing vessels who seek the kingdom; their hearts cry out for the glory God; vessels that will be poured out from glory to glory by the Holy Spirit in the earth. In my glory-view, "the kingdom is an ever-increasing, fruitful, transforming agent in the earth; that is renewing cultures and generations through love by the truth of Christ, operating in men and woman who are steadfastly yielded to God's agenda."

The Lord's people shall speak one to another, "Come, to the house of the Lord that we may learn His ways and obey." The fear of the Lord shall be restored in the house and we will conduct ourselves wisely in the services of the Lord yielding excellent fruit. The order of heaven will come—love, worship, giving, and praise shall be our portion as showers of the heavenly rain falls in the house. Signs and wonders will follow those who believe and restoration will turn into celebration.

After true repentance has taken place and the inner man is being renewed, praise to God will come from a pure heart and that praise will transform into consuming worship. It will be praise that is exhibited with power ushering in the outpour of God's glory. It will be creative praise that will rise above the intensity of perplexing situations. Praise, will give glory to God; help to promote you; reestablish your thoughts; stimulate you to remember what God has done; will lift the fatigued; release fresh energy; baffle the enemy; and inspire you to pay your vows.

"Therefore by Him let us continually offer the sacrifice of praise to God, that is, the fruit of our lips, giving thanks to His name" (Hebrews 13:15).

Where it looked like things were stifled before, motivation will spring back for you to continue on because when one is refreshed they receive strength to fulfill their part of responsibility to the Lord. For responsibility and restoration do coexists. Many of you have made vows to the Lord when you were in the fire, so now that you're out and have been dipped into the pool, go assemble yourself in the sanctuary of God and give Him what is due. David sincerely said in Psalm 66:13-14: *"I will go into your house with burnt offerings; I will pay You my vows, which my lips have uttered and my mouth has spoken when I was in trouble."*

I know that the pool has been an animated and delightful place, but time will come when we will need to go from the pool to pursue our Father's business, so don't stay there too long. My last statement reminds me of the account in the book of St. John, where the sick man who had been in his condition for thirty-eight years, waited for the stirring of the waters by the pool of Bethesda. The word *"Bethesda"* in the Hebrew means, "house of outpouring". This man waited season after season for someone to put him in, but someone always stepped in before him. Jesus came by, saw the man, and asked, "Will you be made whole?" (John 5:1-8).

What a question to ask someone knowing their debilitating condition, knowing that the person wants to come out of his or her dilemma. Was Jesus being facetious? Certainly not! This question, I believe, was intended to provoke in the man the initiative to get up by faith at the command of the Word. In addition to that, Jesus question could have been addressed not only to his physical being, but also to the man's state of mind. If you notice the man's first answer to Jesus' question was not a basic yes or no, instead he commented, "I have no man to put me into the pool when the water is stirred up…" I wonder how many times was this thought rehearsed. Was this his daily bread?

Today, Jesus still poses the same question to us despite of the longevity of the circumstance. He goes pass our "drama" and asks: "Will you be made whole?" If the answer is yes, then Christ has the power to change you on contact. My friend God's refreshing presence is here to heal, save, set free from bondage, revive, bless, and so much more. The living waters are incited; the table is spread and all things are ready. Be encouraged, and be restored from the crown of your head to the soles of your feet. It's your turn!

CHAPTER NINE

Meet for the Master's Use

Therefore if anyone cleanses himself from the later, he will be a vessel for honor,
sanctified and useful for the Master, prepared for every good work.
(II Timothy 2:21)

It came to pass in the previous story, that Mr. Will B. Dunn had completed the process and was ready to be presented to Boss for his up-most service. The story illustrated that before God can position us for service, He must prepare us to stand. Stand in the face of adversity; stand while being challenged to reach another dimension; stand in the midst of men's judgmental actions coming across at you; when you have done all to stand–stand anyhow! Apostle Peter announces to the saints, *"But may the God of all grace, who called us to His eternal glory by Christ Jesus, after you have suffered a while, perfect, establish, strengthen, and settle you" (I Peter 5:10).* This is the time when the scales are removed from our eyes and we can now see clearly many of the things God was doing all along.

On this level, the fleshly fight is not in rule but the "good fight of faith" is. Even though the fight was fixed from the beginning, we still had to step into the invisible ring for the manifestation and the demonstration of the victory. We have learned to allow the Helper to be our guide and fulfill His mission in our life. Not only does He have possession of us but we also have taken a firm hold on Him. We are more attentive to His ongoing handiwork in our life, while we enjoy the privilege of being in His presence. Collectively, everything that we have experienced, the sorrow and the joy has paved the way for us to be broken before Him.

Brokenness is a state of constant systematic refinements of ones will being reshaped to serve the purpose of God reflecting His heart to people on the earth. With this in mind, brokenness doesn't begin when you arrive to church and end when the benediction is

61

stated. Rather, it begins when the heart is tenderized by the Spirit and by obedience to the commandments of Christ. When one is broken, it gives God access to have free course in their life as they abandon themselves wholly unto the Lord. Brokenness produces a flowing humility towards God in surrendering to His desire for you.

When one has come through the fire and is walking in a refined state their hearts cry is, "Your will be done"! We understand that He alone is the Source of life and our dependency on Him has deepened. Not only will we not let the "wages of sin" separate us from God, but we won't tolerate the hardship of circumstances to put a wedge between us either. His enduring love taught us to trust Him. A settling has taken place in our soul and change, although uncomfortable at times, will not easily intimidate us. Momentum has been established through the Word and will be maintained as we continue to grow up and beyond; simply put, being led by the Spirit of God.

Growing Up and Beyond

Because God's grace is sufficient, it gives us room to grow. Ephesians 4:15 declares, *"But speaking the truth in love, may grow up in all things into Him who is the head—Christ."* Growth is a product of choice and cultivation. The enemy of the soul hates for the believer to grow. He knows that without spiritual growth, stagnation and darkness will settle in. As long as breath is in our bodies, opportunities for growth are inexhaustible. We who are in the body of Christ have come through great struggles, but don't stop reaching. Keep growing up and beyond, increasing in the knowledge of God, and eating the meat of Christ's maturity. In her book, *Water my Soul*, Luci Shaw penned: **"Be on the alert for the kind of growth in your soul that pleases God—growth in grace, in wisdom, in love, whether it comes fast, like the front lawn, or with agonizing slowness, like the oak tree."**

Notice that a child doesn't struggle to grow, they just grow. Well, we don't have to struggle to grow, because being "partakers of the divine nature" of Christ ensures our growth: a growth that takes us beyond confirmation into action. Also, a child not only out grows his or her clothes and toys but they reach or cross over to maturity. They go beyond their parent's house into their own; beyond high school into college; beyond playmates on to marriage, they want to spread their wings. And that's what the Spirit is saying to us—stretch out and expand your wings to new horizons spiritually and naturally. His grace works holy influence over us enabling us to add to our faith (see II Peter 3:3-7).

Grace carries the power to assist us not only in the work of the Lord but in our every day lives. It's a blessing to know that daily "we can find grace to help in the time of need." Whether it is in something large or small, I need the assistance of grace moment by moment. We are admonished to *"grow in grace and in the knowledge of the Lord and Savior Jesus Christ"* (II Peter 3:18). The more we receive insight, light, and revelation through the Scriptures by the Holy Spirit, we also receive grace for grace to be like Him.

The grace of God is also a teacher and as we continue to learn of Him, we will with competence reach beyond the "SOS" (same old stuff) because our spiritual appetite has changed and is calling for more. I don't know about you, but when I'm hungry my mind goes on a quick taste bud search to see what I want to eat. It's hunger on a mission to enjoy and digest the food that I've been craving for. I believe that hunger leads to searching, searching to finding, found to action, and action to fulfillment. The intensity of hunger, the God-kind of hunger, is to serve the full intentions of the will of God. Hunger is not driven by circumstances but it is a willing desire that prepensely stays connected to the Glory Source that subsequently keeps us asking for more. Spiritual hunger is born out of intimacy with the Father and keeps you awakened to the power of discovery and gives the ability to bring successful resolve. Jesus taught in Matthew 5:6, *"Blessed are those who do hunger and thirst after righteousness, for they shall be filled."*

It's Praying Time

Cultivating a praying foundation, seals in the freshness. While we proceed forward, stirring up the gift of God within us, it's also necessary that we maintain the ground that we have gained by utilizing the tool of prayer.

Prayer in its simplest definition is: communing with God, being in union with God. It is an interaction of humbly beseeching God with a sincere heart. I like to think of prayer as a "spiritual business transaction" because as I sow into prayer I reap potent results both naturally and spiritually, that prepares me to fulfill the will of God in my daily life. Prayer is also a "wireless" communication that is lucrative to the inner-man and a life outreach to other men called, **intercession.**

> *"And I sought for a man among them, that should make up the hedge, and stand in the gap before me for the land, that I should not destroy it: but I found none"* (Ezekiel 22:30 KJV).

Jesus, our great High Priest, ever lives to make intercession for us. (See Hebrews 7:25). It is His desire that we enter into His intercession, as different ones are laid upon our hearts. Intercession is rooted in the love of God. It is a life-giving force that will not relinquish its assignment until God's purpose is executed. Therefore, it is difficult to truly stand in the gap for someone you don't care about. I have found out that genuine concern for others builds a hedge of safety for them to confess their faults and be healed (James 5:16). It's something about intercession that allows us to take a break from ourselves and give attention to others who are in need. When we pray for others and contribute to their necessity, God will intervene on your behalf.

Intercession is crafted to under-gird people by faith and grace. With so much happening in the body of Christ today, many are finding themselves in pivotal places, needing intercession to help them crossover to will of God for their lives. For those who are held captive by Satan in darkness, intercession is a targeted weapon with a mission to release the souls to the light of God's power. Yes, the vocation of intercession will cost us a life of sacrifice, but every soul is worth it! May we ponder this in our hearts today to be a representative and stand in the gap (**G**o **A**nd **P**ray).

> *"But seek first the kingdom of God and His righteousness, and all these things shall be added to you"* (Matthew 6:33).

The art of prayer is ongoing—it works both now and later. The word picture of prayer may change from day to day and the color of your circumstances may vary; but Jesus, the Master Artist, whom we pray to is always the same. Prayer is not the end just because it was answered, but rather it is a door of expansion taking place in you to experience more of the manifested life of Christ. Prayer is not a leisure that we partake of **if** we have time; rather, it is a graceful diligence that we **must take time** to do. The Scriptures informs us, *"So He Himself* {Jesus} *often withdrew into the wilderness and prayed"* (Luke 5:16). *"And when He had sent the multitudes away, He went up on a mountain by Himself to pray. And when evening had come He was alone there"* (Matthew 14:23).

Jesus, was responsible in attending the services of the altar. He saw it as urgent worship, being fully present in mind, girded for action, and by no means willing to let the fire of the altar go out! His prayers were always sober and equivalent to the intensity of the demand at hand.

> *"You are to be responsible for the care of the sanctuary and the altar, so that My wrath will not fall on the Israelites again"* (Numbers 18:5). NIV

The sacred historical altar of God is a place where order is valued and was built and kept in trust for the authenticity of three core values:

Worship	**Relates to**	**Acceptable Sacrifice**
Willingness	**Relates to**	**Graceful Surrender**
Wholeness	**Relates to**	**Redemptive Soundness**

Choosing to bear these precious values in our hearts will always lead us to an open altar, restoring the cry within to reach out to the Living God.

When one is dedicated to God in prayer, prayer in turn will protect your dedication. However, praylessness causes roadblocks to be set up against sensitivity to the Holy Spirit. No prayer will not only leave you unprotected, it will inevitably leave you powerless.

We can see in our country the tragic repercussions of violence and decadence when prayer is taken out of the schools, homes, and in some cases—the church! The devil knows that his time isn't much longer and his attacks are increasing. If we allow him to steal away our prayer commitment, <u>one</u> of our weapons of defense is gone. Isn't it interesting how that churches all over the country can conduct a musical or theater play and the house will be packed out; but let them announce prayer, only a few will show up and the rest will be missing "Without a Trace".

> *"Moreover the word of the Lord came unto Jeremiah a second time, while he was still shut up in the court of the prison, saying, "Thus says the Lord who made it, the Lord who formed it to establish it (the Lord is His name): Call unto Me, and I will answer you, and show you great and might things, which you do not know"* (Jeremiah 33:1-3).

It's good to know that the Word of the Lord has no boundaries. It possesses the capability to find us anywhere at anytime. You may be shut up in prison like Jeremiah, one of the major prophets who was persecuted for speaking God's Word. You may be in a hospital, nursing home, hurtful relationship, or just in a hard place, but wherever you are you can pour out your heart to God. Talk to Him about everything. Mark Littleton said, "Turn your doubts to questions; turn your questions to prayers; turn you prayers to God."

God urges His people to call unto Him. He will show us secret things, which we have not known. How will this be revealed? The Spirit will reveal it through prayer and the Word. The Spirit specializes in prayer. The Scripture unfolds to us: *"Likewise the Spirit also helps in our weakness. For we do not know what we should pray for as we ought, but the Spirit Himself makes intercession for us with groanings which cannot be uttered"* (Romans 8:26). KJV Spending time with the Lord is imperative. Get in His presence to worship and love on Him. His Spirit will impart to us what we need from moment to moment. Even when you can't seem to "feel" His presence at a particular time, keep on praying with an assured heart that He is near. Don't go after the feeling—go after Him. It is a blessed privilege to have this invitation and to know that: *"Now this is the confidence that we have in Him, that if we ask anything according to will, He hears us. And if we know that He hears us, whatever we ask, we know that we have the petitions that we have asked of Him"* (I John 5:14-15).

Jesus gave us an example and pattern to the prayer life we should have. His prayer in Gethsemane, *"Saying, Father, if it is your will, remove this cup from Me; nevertheless not My will, but Yours be done. And be being in agony, He prayed more earnestly. And His sweat became like great drops of blood falling down to the ground"* (Luke 22:42,44). My dear sisters and brothers, the pressures of some agonizing situations may be all around you right now, but be consistent in prayer. Keep your heart open for fellowship with the Lord. Abiding in the secret place with the Father, will render us to be effective and refreshed. He wants to wrap us in His glory and present us as a gift to His Body.

Let us come together to rebuild the consecrated altars unto the Lord. All those who will stand in the gap will adhere to the call and "weep between the porch and the altar" (Joel 2:17). The Intercessors will be broken before the Lord, to receive His burden and go to the places where they have been assigned. He did not say that He didn't have any burden but that *"My yoke is easy and My burden is light"* (Matthew 11:30).

Sign on the Dotted Line

When we become of age, life summons us to some committed obligation's that require a signature. This signature should denote a binding agreement that the person(s) adheres to whatever is stated in a particular document. If the signature is presented but there is no compliance to that which has been signed, it is then considered a "breach of contract".

Paul expressed in I Corinthians 13:11: *"When I was a child, I spoke as a child, I understood as a child, I thought as a child; but when I became a man, I put away childish things."* I want you to look at the last part of the Scripture, "I put away childish things." Take the first letter of each word, put them together and you will come with the word p-a-c-t. According to *Webster's Dictionary,* this word *pact* indicates: an agreement between persons, a covenant. The above Scripture in context with previous verses 1-10 is speaking of the more excellent way, which is love. God is love. And through love He sent us the Seal of His signature, Jesus Christ, to bind us by His blood covenant forever to Him. Growing up in the Lord motivates us to agree with Him in thought and action. It is His plans that we must comply with and His plans always involve His choice.

> *"There are many plans in a man's heart, nevertheless the Lord's counsel—that will stand"* (Proverbs 19:21).

The covenant of the Lord is already established. We don't have to add or subtract from it, just walk in it. To walk in covenant is to acquire the knowledge of God and learn to sacrifice. Sacrificing is a series of offerings of giving up one thing for the sake of another. It is a performance of love as it relates to value, because whatever or whoever we value, we will without hesitation make sacrifices for. Truly, the Lord is worthy! He is worthy of our spiritual signature (vows made unto the Lord), praise, time, finances, effort, ect… He is precious and His value is above all else, in heaven and earth. Because He first valued us much more than the birds of the air, (see Luke 12:24) certainly, we should value Him.

In my studying of the Old Testament Sacrificial System, I found out that everything was especially prepared in order unto the Lord. Certain animals were assigned to different offerings. For example, the bullocks were assigned to the Burnt offering and the Sin offering. (See Leviticus 1:5-17 and 4:1-35). The Burnt offering mostly symbolized a complete consecrated life unto God. The bullock's blood was drained and his body was cut into pieces and laid in order upon the altar to be consumed by fire as a whole Burnt offering. Only God can take something that was broken and make it whole again. Even as Christ's body was broken for us, He sacrificed His life that we may be made whole. God said, *"Gather my saints together unto me, those that have a covenant with me by sacrifice"* (Psalms 50:5).

Now today we are not required to offer up animal sacrifices, but God is asking for a devoted and consecrated life for the cause of Christ. He wants every part of us laid upon the altar—spirit, soul, and body. He will send His anointed fire to consume us that we may present unto Him offerings of righteousness. Let me encourage you while I encourage myself to respond to the redemptive covenant, and reach our purpose in Christ. I implore you, please sign here. _____

"I beseech you therefore brethren, by the mercies of God, that you present your bodies a living sacrifice, holy, acceptable to God which is your reasonable service" (Romans 12:1).

Lord, Use Me.

I'm convinced that if there has ever been a time to affect our generation it is now! We carry within us blessings and favor for our generation. Apostle Paul states in his preaching concerning David, *"For David, after he had served his own generation by the will of God, fell asleep, and was laid unto his fathers, and saw corruption:"* (Acts 13:36). During his life span King David made such an impact on people through his relationship with God that hundred's of years later enriches and impels us to this day.

The Lord greatly used David in getting things accomplished for His glory. Now when I speak of the word "**use**" I don't mean it in terms of abuse or taking advantage through greedy motives for ones own personal gain. Instead, I think of two industrious words: **productive** and **profitable.**

In the life of David the Lord anointed him to be productive. He brought forth qualitative results that were fruitful and extensible to the kingdom. Although he wasn't a perfect man, his diligence and devotion was making him a man of principal. While he steadfastly mixed the Word with faith, his availability and willingness to God promoted him to the throne at the appointed time.

Since David committed his works unto the Lord, he profitably advanced in a sound yet unusual way that evoked enlightenment and prosperity to him and others. No assignment given to him was beneath him because he knew who he was. He understood that "in labor there is profit, but idle chatter leads only to proverty" (Proverbs 14:23). To every assignment there is a strategy, but when given by the Lord, there is significance and victory attached to it.

"Thus says the Lord, your Redeemer, the Holy One of Israel: "I am the Lord your God, Who teaches you to profit, Who leads you by the way you should go" (Isaiah 48:17).

Now when I come to the throne of grace and unpretentiously ask the Lord to use me, I meditate on God working the meaning of these two words in all the measure of my life. I want to be able to qualitatively express myself as God's witness of His awesome power and saving grace. That's why bathing ourselves in the Word is so relevant in order to be sanctified and useful for the Master.

You and I are capable believers "created in Christ Jesus unto good works". "You Are Wanted"! Someone needs you! You are significant and have something to offer. God has not called us to sit on the bench of "do nothing". Your God-given dreams and visions have not been forgotten, so please don't abort them! You cannot afford to go "A-Wall" on your assignment; the vision will come to pass. The vision or dream may have been undergoing a period of cultivation, a proving time, which will eventually allow that vision to evolve to the forefront.

Our faith in God, through the difficulties of life may have actually caused the vision or dream to enlarge. He's allowing our myopic self-centered world to unravel like the loose threads of a garment. Ever notice that as thread unwinds, the hem in the material expands? Take a moment to think on that. And while you are thinking, go ahead and give God praise even when it appears like things are fallen apart. Could it be that the Lord is reorganizing to make room for you in an appointed place?

Sometimes in the labor of a beginning vision we may start off alone like being on a secret mission as we work toward accomplishing it. But inevitably the fruit and function of that vision will be shared. Others will partake of the pleasing bonus of your obedience. A couple of years ago, a friend asked to me to aid her with a project she was working on. And while helping her with her vision, I realized that I had been willing to do for her what I wouldn't do for myself. Nevertheless, in my willingness to support her, it gave me insight to my own potential. And as I began to set my heart and my hands to the work, my gift was stirred up.

"Now unto Him who is able to do exceedingly abundantly above all that we ask or think, according to the power that works in us" (Ephesians 3:20).

God has made us fit and equipped for His glory as we give ourselves unto the Lord and render service to the people, being an example in love. To God our availability is a treasure; it is a direct link to a kingdom response that honors "The Beginning of the Creation of God." There are some in the number who have made up their minds not to succumb to the mediocrity of "church-ism" but contrary wise, will by the Spirit, move gallantly to their valid destiny in the army of the Lord. They know and attest in their spirits that the "best is yet to come"! It's not over! What then is the conclusion? I find it in the words of the prophet Isaiah, *"Also I heard the voice of the Lord, saying, Whom shall I send, and who will for us? Then said I, Here am I; send me"* (Isaiah 6:8).

Prayer:

Father, here we stand take hold of our hand. Wash us in Your blood anew, help us to reflect Your love being vessels of honor for You. We can't do it on our own, only through Christ can the light be shown. You never said the journey would be easy, so put strength in our souls and give us courage to be bold. Direct our hearts in Your ways and let us not error from the truth of Your Word. So much is happening in the world, and we must admit that at times we are overwhelmed. Nevertheless, we look to You, Oh Rock of Ages, for You know exactly what to do. Lord crown us with Your goodness; for we delight in praising You. Guide us until the day is done as we thank You for the victory already won. Use us Lord, Thy kingdom come. This we pray in Jesus name, Amen.

For more information, please contact the author at
email address:cgardglory@gmail.com